# THE
# COMEBACK

D0027181

How Larry Ellison's Team
Won the America's Cup

G. Bruce Knecht

Previously published material. *The Wall Street Journal*: articles by the author published on Feb. 5, 2002, May 26, 2005, June 2, 2005, May 10, 2006, Nov. 4, 2006, April 18, 2007, July 9, 2010, and Oct. 23, 2010. *Showboats Magazine*: article by the author published in March 2008. *Rhapsody* Magazine: article by the author published in March 2014.

*Printed in the United States of America*

ISBN-13: 978-1532994203

ISBN-10: 1532994206

Cover and interior design by
Charles Rue Woods

# THE
# COMEBACK

*For Alex*

Hvala Bogu,...
Lovely setting,
Lovely people.
Totally
memorable.
THEO

A thrilling
trip and a
most welcome
arrival in
the end
Geof

Next time come
by car...
Andy

# CONTENTS

# Prologue

Even when he's relaxed, Sir Russell Coutts looks intense. With his steely gaze and powerful jaw, it's difficult to imagine him in any organization where he isn't in a position of authority. And right now, on a beautiful afternoon in September 2013, the sailor in charge of Larry Ellison's America's Cup campaign—Oracle Team USA—was nowhere near relaxed. He was well beyond agitated, on his way to profanity-inflected tantrum.

Coutts was aboard a high-speed chase boat hurtling across San Francisco Bay when Oracle's catamaran, an all-black vessel that looked more starship than sailboat, attempted to round a mark while staying up on its hydrofoils—four slender, carbon-fiber appendages that sprouted from the bottom of the boat to make it possible to levitate the rest of the vessel above the water. It was a challenging maneuver, one the team had never attempted in a race before. And it didn't work. The hulls crashed into the water, and the flying boat suddenly turned into something closer to a snowplow.

"What the *fuck* was that?" Coutts shouted. Before the maneuver, which had been called for by John Kostecki, Oracle's tactician, Oracle had been leading the race, the fifth in the series. Now, in seconds, Team New Zealand closed the gap, then seized the lead. Coutts looked like he was going to explode. Over and over he asked, *"Why the fuck did he do that?"*

*Oracle Team USA Trails Team New Zealand.*

New Zealand quickly built a 1,500-meter lead as they rocketed toward another win, which raised its total to 4 and left Oracle at minus 1. Yes, *minus 1*. Ellison's team had been caught making illegal modifications to its boat in a preliminary round of racing. Three veteran crewmembers had been banned from racing for the duration of the Cup. And there was another penalty: Oracle would start the first-to-nine competition for the greatest prize in sailing with minus 2 points. Oracle had not even made it to zero.

Ellison, a hypercompetitive high-tech mogul unaccustomed to losing, was watching the self-destruction of his America's Cup dream from another chase boat, which had delivered him to the racecourse from his 288-foot-long Feadship-built power yacht, *Musashi*. The yacht served as a hulking reminder of his vast wealth and the kind of resources that were available to his team. Named for a Samurai swordsman who is said to have fought more than sixty duels without a defeat, *Musashi* is fitted out with the kind of amenities you might expect on a vessel that cost about as much as Ellison's campaign for the Cup, something more than $200 million: elegant wood-paneled compartments, a gym and a hair salon, a cinema, engines that can generate 14,600 horsepower to transport Ellison and his twenty-three-person crew at twenty-two knots. There is even space for a helicopter hangar that is concealed below deck and a "garage" for a pair of tenders almost large enough to be called yachts in their own right.

Ellison was born to an unwed mother who gave him up for adoption and raised in a small apartment on the

South Side of Chicago. His adoptive father, who took his name from Ellis Island, repeatedly told Larry he would not amount to much. And, in fact, for many years the prediction seemed accurate. Ellison was uninterested in school or organized sports, and he didn't like being told what to do by anyone. But somewhere along the line he became insatiably ambitious. Many years later, when I asked him whether that came from knowing that his mother had given him up, he paused, which was unusual, and locked his eyes on mine before he acknowledged the impact with humor. "Well," he said, "I wouldn't recommend it as a strategy."

After taking classes but not graduating from the University of Illinois and the University of Chicago, where he learned to write computer code, Ellison drove a beat-up car to California. None of his earliest jobs lasted very long, but when he heard about a new kind of software that could store and manipulate very large databases, his restless energies found focus and, in 1977, he founded a company that would become Oracle Corporation. It would make him one of the world's richest men, but even that was not nearly enough, so he also sought out arenas outside of business in which he could compete.

The idea that he might win the America's Cup had been particularly tantalizing, and, after two unsuccessful attempts, in 2010 he became the first American to do so since 1992 by defeating the Swiss team led by Ernesto Bertarelli, the reigning champion, in Spain. Ellison was ecstatic. When I suggested that winning the Cup might end up being his most enduring achievement, more important than Oracle Corporation, the first line of his obituary, he did not disagree. "Oracle could just disappear someday," he said. "The America's Cup will not."

Winning the Cup gave Ellison the right to bring the competition to San Francisco, his home base since the early 1970s, and to create an outrageous new class of boats that had received widespread skepticism before the start of the racing. But his yachting achievements would be greatly diminished if he ended up losing by a lopsided score in front of a hometown audience. California's richest man, a goliath in global commerce and a powerful presence in American society, had unexpectedly become the underdog—and he was not about to accept this sudden change of fortune without a fight. Even before Team New Zealand crossed the finish line, he called Coutts. The message was curt, and simple.

"You need to make some changes," he said, "or we're going down."

The changes started at once, in hours snatched from between races—perhaps the most intensive re-engineering effort in the long history of the Cup. Engineers designed and fabricated through the night. The alterations would be both technical and tactical. They would also involve the use of a sailing technique that was prohibited under the rules. But the odds were lined up against Ellison. Team New Zealand had the faster boat and it was riding a powerful, seemingly unstoppable wave of momentum.

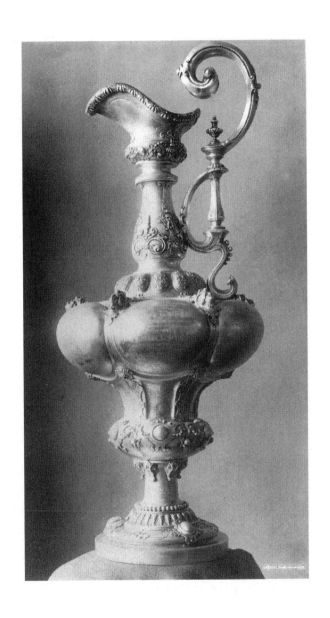

# God and Larry Ellison

The America's Cup has its unlikely beginnings in the summer of 1851 when a schooner built by several wealthy New Yorkers arrived in England for a race around the Isle of Wight. Whether it was warships or yachts, England was the predominant master of the seas, so it was an audacious challenge. So too was the New Yorkers' vessel. Named *America,* its pointed bow, broad stern and severely raked masts gave it a very different look from other racing yachts of the day, leading one prominent British yachtsman, Henry Paget, 1st Marquis of Anglesey, to declare, "If she is right, then all of us are wrong." On August 22, *America* was proved right as she circumnavigated the island faster than fourteen English vessels.

*America*'s owners were rewarded with an ornate silver ewer, which they named "The America's Cup" and presented to the New York Yacht Club with the understanding that it would become a perpetual prize for a "friendly competition between foreign countries." The Cup now stands as the oldest continuously active trophy in international sport, which is one of the reasons it has drawn the interest of extraordinarily wealthy Americans from J.P. Morgan and two generations of Vanderbilts to, more recently, quirky mavericks like Ted Turner, Bill Koch, and Ellison.

Some of the foreign contenders have been equally colorful: Sir Thomas Lipton, the tea and retailing magnate; Baron Bich, the flamboyant aristocrat who struck gold with his disposable Bic pens; and Alan Bond, who was named Australian of the Year after he broke the New York Yacht Club's 132-year stranglehold over the Cup in 1983 but was later declared bankrupt, convicted of fraud, and sent to prison.

The winning team gains temporary possession of the Cup along with the right to make most of the decisions about the next contest. New technology and less-than-sportsmanlike behavior have always been part of the mix, but the competition in San Francisco involved technological advances and misconduct—some of it proven, some merely alleged, and some that would go unnoticed—far more dramatic than anything that had come before.

\* \* \* \*

For Ellison, the Cup involved all of his most motivating hot buttons: competition, money, and the application of radically disruptive technologies. When I spoke to him shortly before he wrested the Cup from Ernesto Bertarelli, the Swiss billionaire, in 2010, Ellison said the opportunity for personal participation—he was a member of the sailing crew during that regatta—had also driven his pursuit. "I could buy the New York Yankees, but I couldn't play shortstop," was how he put it.

*Larry Ellison*

Several years earlier, Ellison told me that he views life as an endless experiment aimed at determining just how good he can be in a great diversity of endeavors. Whether it's making money, racing boats, piloting stunt planes, acquiring spectacular homes, or playing tennis, Ellison has always rated himself rather highly, a point emphasized by the unconventional title of biographer Mike Wilson's book *The Difference Between God and Larry Ellison*. (The subtitle proposed an answer: "God Doesn't Think He's Larry Ellison.") The book describes a career built on ever-expanding ambitions and outrageous business moves accompanied by ruthlessness, egotistical abandon, and astonishing personal reinvention.

One of the other themes of Ellison's life is a ceaseless quest for speed. In addition to his boats and pushing Oracle Corporation employees to produce ever-faster software and to sell it more quickly, Ellison owns an array of high-performance planes and cars. "There are two aspects of speed," Ellison told me. "One is the absolute notion of speed. Then there's the relative notion—trying to go faster than the next guy. I think it's the latter that's much more interesting. It's an expression of our primal being. Ever since we were living in villages as hunter-gatherers, great rewards went to people who were stronger, faster."

\* \* \* \*

No one was surprised when Ellison decided that America's Cup competitors would sail giant catamarans rather than traditional single-hull vessels in 2013. Because two hulls provide the natural stability of a raft, catamarans do not need heavy keels to counteract the force of the wind against the sails (or wing). Therefore, they can be lighter and have less water resistance—and be substantially faster.

Under the design parameters that were devised by Coutts and endorsed by Ellison, each competitor could build two catamarans that were seventy-two feet long and up to forty-six feet wide. They would be powered by 131-foot-high wings rather than traditional sails.

Traditionalists were horrified by the seventy-two-foot-long monsters that resulted. The AC72s, as they became known, didn't even look like boats, and the eleven crewmen who sailed them didn't look like yachtsmen. They wore helmets and the kind of impact-resistant clothing used by motorcycle racers, and they carried oxygen canisters to sustain themselves in the event of a capsize—an ever-present danger. In their high-tech fittings the crew resembled a legion of superheroes, particularly when the boats turned through the breeze and the sailors rushed from one hull by bounding across the "platform," trampoline-like webbing about the size of a tennis court, to reach the other.

Ellison's level of personal involvement would be far smaller than it had been in 2010, in part because the boats required a level of athleticism unlike any previous Cup regatta. Ellison still wrote the checks, spoke regularly to Coutts, and he would show up for races, but that was about it. And yet, in another sense his aspirations had become more expansive than ever. In addition to winning, Ellison wanted to transform an event that had significant name recognition but little spectator interest into a full-fledged international sporting franchise, like Wimbledon or Formula One.

To do this, Ellison wanted the racing to be visible from shore rather than far off the coast, which is where most Cups had been sailed. He talked about "stadium sailing," which was actually possible given San Francisco's steady breezes and the natural amphitheater that surrounds the bay. Even more important, he wanted to attract substantial television audiences, and that would be impossible unless the boats were fast.

The AC72 met that final standard with ease. With its pair of narrow hulls and thirteen-story-high wing, its hulls could lift out of the water and ride on its hydrofoils—one could be lowered from the center of each of the hulls; the other two were attached to the rudders—to eliminate much of the water's drag and reach speeds upwards of fifty miles per hour. That was *four times* faster than America's Cup yachts of just a decade ago (and twice as fast as the mighty *Musashi* with its four diesel engines at full tilt).

To ensure that the event would comport with television schedules, there would be two races a day, each of which had to be completed within forty minutes, a big change from previous Cup regattas in which races often took three hours or more. This time if a race could not be completed in forty minutes it would be abandoned. The racecourse, which would be the same in every race, would include two three-mile downwind legs and an upwind sprint of equal length on a racecourse compressed between Alcatraz Island and the city's shoreline.

The sailing itself would also be radically different from previous America's Cup races. Manipulating the wings, foils, and rudders required a daunting combination of traditional sailing smarts, lightning-fast decision-making, and pure brawn. Even communication was challenging. When the AC72 moved at thirty miles an hour into a twenty-mile-per-hour breeze, conditions that were not unusual, the result was a deafening roar no different from what would happen if you were to stick your head out the window of a speeding car. Jimmy Spithill, the super-charged Australian redhead who was helming Oracle's boat, could speak to the crew by helmet-mounted microphone, which transmitted to speakers inside everyone's helmets, but the helmets made ordinary talking difficult. They blocked nearby voices but not the thunderous sound of the wind.

*The crew wore helmets and impact-resistant clothing.*

With speed came considerable danger, which represented a surprising twist for Ellison. He had given up ocean racing and turned to the America's Cup after his own life was jeopardized when he participated in the 1998 Sydney to Hobart Race. The fleet had sailed into a powerful cyclone. Of the 115 boats that started the race, only forty-three crossed the finish line. Several sank. Five men ended up on a flimsy life raft that was repeatedly overturned until three of them were swept away by an enormous wave. Before the storm had passed, three other sailors also died.

When I interviewed Ellison for my book about the disaster, *The Proving Ground: The Inside Story of the 1998 Sydney to Hobart Race,* he said, "This is not what racing is supposed to be. Difficult, yes. Dangerous, no." He said he would continue to sail but vowed that he would never again enter a long-distance race in open ocean. "I decided to focus on a more technical and less life-threatening form of sailing," he told me.

But now, by creating this new class of boats, Ellison had made America's Cup sailing more than simply dangerous. Some longtime sailing observers called the AC72s "death traps," overpowered beasts that were always skating on the edge of catastrophe. Almost a year before the start of the Cup, one of Oracle's AC72s flipped and was severely damaged during training. In May 2013, Andrew "Bart" Simpson, a two-time British Olympic medalist, was sailing for Sweden's Artemis Racing—one of several teams that were competing against each other to determine which of them would sail against Oracle for the Cup—when one of the bows of Artemis's AC72 dug deeply into the water, causing the vessel to break apart and capsize. Simpson, the thirty-six-year-old father of two young boys, was trapped beneath the wreckage, and drowned.

# Buying Time

As he watched the failure of Kostecki's maneuver, Russell Coutts may have looked like he was in the grip of uncontrollable rage. But he was already mapping out plans for a potential comeback. To begin with, he intended to take the radical step of playing the team's single "postponement card" to cancel the second race of the day. The card was designed to give teams an opportunity to avoid forfeiting a race because of boat problems, but Coutts wanted to play it for a different reason: to buy time.

"We have to unscramble what the hell they're doing," he said, referring to Team New Zealand. "They're sailing in a completely different mode."

Others on the chase boat thought playing the postponement card now was a terrible idea. Grant Simmer, a veteran Australian sailor who was Oracle Team USA's general manager, asked, "What happens when we have a breakage later on?"

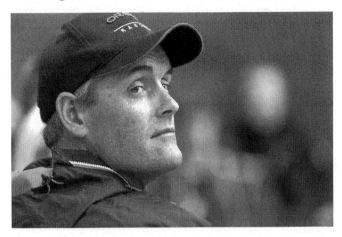

*Russell Coutts*

Coutts shook his head. At the rate Oracle was going, there probably wouldn't be a later on. "It's simple math," he declared." If we sail the next race, we are *going* to lose it. If we have a breakdown later, we *might* lose a race."

Coutts always attacked problems head on. He had shocked the rest of the team's leadership when he said he wanted to play the postponement card after Oracle lost the very first race and again after they came up short in the third. On those occasions, he had been rebuffed by Spithill, whose hypercompetitive nature made him uncomfortable with anything that might look like a retreat. Coutts didn't want to overrule his skipper, but this time he would insist. When Oracle crossed the finish line after the disastrous snowplow, thirty-six excruciating seconds behind New Zealand, Coutts's chase boat sped to the catamaran. Coutts, who had by then taken the wheel, asked Spithill to come aboard and told the other passengers to move to the back of the boat so he could have a private conversation.

This time there was no disagreement. Spithill had independently decided that it was time to play the postponement card. It was a momentous decision but Ellison didn't hear about it until afterward.

Coutts and Spithill also agreed that the tactician, John Kostecki, the earnest San Francisco native who was one of only two Americans on the supposedly American team, had to be replaced. Even before the disastrous maneuver, Coutts had been unhappy with his performance. "A lot of sports is about confidence," he later told me. "JK was having a lousy regatta."

The postponement was announced just before 3:00 p.m. on Tuesday, September 10. There would be no second race that afternoon and Wednesday was a scheduled day off from racing. The next contest would begin on Thursday at 1:00 p.m., giving Oracle almost two full days to reinvent itself.

The sailors returned to Oracle's home base, a sprawling waterfront warehouse that was painted black and was so large that some of the team's 200 employees used bicycles to get around. A who's who of marine experts from around the world that included thirty-two boat builders and riggers, they lived all over the city, but they had spent most of the previous three years at the base, which operated around the clock and was protected by tall fences and security guards whose uniforms were also all black.

After every day of sailing, the AC72 was plucked from the water by a crane and the wing and the hulls were taken inside, separately, by specially designed transporters. Even if no physical changes were made to the boat, it took dozens of people just to remove and inspect systems to insure everything was working perfectly. The activity level was always high, but like a high-tech factory or a Bond villain's lair, everything in the warehouse was meticulously organized and spotlessly clean.

*Oracle's AC72 was taken inside every day.*

Some areas did not feel like a factory, particularly the sailing team's physical fitness center, which had everything you would find in a high-quality gym along with whiteboards filled with data related to the team's rigorous training programs. Not far away, a pair of pre-fabricated structures had been set up inside the warehouse. One functioned as a lounge and cafeteria—a carpeted space with sliding glass doors instead of walls, several cappuccino machines, and couches where members of the shore crew watched the racing on television. The other structure housed offices for Coutts, senior members of the sailing team, and designers. That building was less comfortable. Many of its inhabitants were being lavishly compensated, but the furniture and lighting fixtures were cheap and flimsy, which gave everything a feeling of impermanence.

When Coutts arrived, he spoke to Oracle's sailing coach, a dynamic Frenchman named Philippe Presti, about replacing Kostecki. Both men knew it was a risky move. Maybe even desperate. Coutts was a student of America's Cup history and he frequently pointed out that no contender that had swapped out a key crewmember had ever gone on to win, but now he wanted to do just that. Presti thought Coutts himself should be the replacement. He had been the helmsman for three successful America's Cup campaigns—two from his native New Zealand and one from Switzerland—and won every one of the fourteen Cup races he helmed, more than anyone else in the event's 162-year history, plus an Olympic gold medal. His record and personality came together to endow him with an aura of invincibility.

But Coutts declined. "I'm fifty-one years old," he said, "and I haven't done nearly enough sailing on the boat."

Coutts had a different idea: he wanted to put another sailing superstar, Ben Ainslie, on the boat. A thirty-six-year-old Briton with dark hair and, since the start of the regatta, a thickening beard, Ainslie is a man with two personalities. On land, he is soft spoken and gentle to the point of meek. When I met him for lunch after the racing in San Francisco, it was often difficult to even hear his voice. But on the water, he's ferocious. After a 2011 race in which he believed a press boat had interfered with his sailing and robbed him of a first-place finish, Ainslie dove into the water, swam to the offending boat and launched into a heated discussion that ended with him shoving a photographer before he dove back into the water.

*Ben Ainslie*

With four gold medals and a silver, he is the most successful sailor in Olympic history, and, like Coutts, he had prevailed in so many major regattas that he had been awarded a knighthood. What Ainslie really wanted to do was organize a British effort to finally reclaim the America's Cup, but that would have to wait. He joined

Oracle shortly after the 2012 Olympic Games. He was hired to helm Oracle's second AC72—the "B" boat—during training sessions. Providing Spithill with a challenging sparring partner was important, but it meant he was not a member of the primary sailing squad. He had always sailed against Spithill rather than with him.

* * * *

Steering the AC72 involved the usual helming challenges as well as an entirely different dimension: manipulating six steering-wheel-mounted buttons, which could, when the boat was moving sufficiently fast, alter the angle of the hydrofoils so they would lift the bulk of the seven-ton vessel up out of the water. Jimmy Spithill said it sometimes felt less like sailing than like piloting an airplane or surfing, both of which he did in his spare time.

"If one thing goes out of whack," he told me, "everything falls apart. There is no halfway. Once you commit to a big wave, you can't stop halfway through. And you're always close to the edge." By "close to the edge" he meant "on the verge of capsizing."

Driving the boat was so all-consuming that Spithill had to depend on his tactician to help decide when to turn, what course to take, when to stay close to the competition, when to break away. The helmsman-tactician relationship required not just confidence and trust but seamless communication as well as unspoken understandings. And while Ainslie was thought by many—including Spithill—to be the world's best sailor, he, in addition to not having sailed with Spithill, had never acted as a tactician for another helmsman.

After talking to Presti, Coutts asked Kostecki to meet him and Spithill in his office. Like everyone on Oracle's team, Kostecki had a spectacular résumé. He was, in fact, the only person in sailing history to hold the ultimate trifecta of sailing achievements: winning an Olympic medal, the around-the-world Volvo Ocean Race, and an America's Cup regatta. But he too recognized that he was not having his best regatta. As soon as Coutts said, "We need to make a change," Kostecki signaled his understanding.

"I agree—it's not working," he said, adding, "I want to do whatever is best for the team."

Then Spithill, without Coutts, went to Ainslie's office, who had just one question: "I need to know that you really support this."

"Yeah, I'm comfortable with it," Spithill replied. "We could really use your energy."

# Remaking the Wing

Grant Simmer, the general manager, gathered Oracle's thirty-member design team around a long white table in a common space just outside the offices. "If we don't find ways to improve the boat, we might win a couple races, but we're going to lose the Cup," he told them. When Coutts, whose academic credentials include an engineering degree, joined the meeting, he made a specific demand: "I want to have six ideas in an hour." The boat's primary source of power—the wing—was the obvious focal point.

From a telegenic distance the wing appeared metallic and solid, but most of its outer surfaces were made from plastic film not much thicker than Saran wrap. The

*The "solid" wings were actually pliable.*

wing was also far more complicated than its appearance suggested. While it looked like a single object and was referred to as "rigid," it was in fact neither. The interior structure was made with horizontal frames that were a couple of feet wide and two inches thick but weighed almost nothing. The sides of each of the frames were made from thin layers of carbon fiber, but the inside was comprised of corrugated paper. And the wing had many pieces, including four separate vertical elements, each composed of four horizontal sections that could be manipulated independently. Much more than an airplane wing, it was a pliable instrument.

The wing's adaptability had given rise to a revolutionary possibility that the designers and sailors had only begun to recognize: with a complicated ballet of maneuvers, it could begin to replicate the magnificent dynamism of the beating wing of a bird. The most crucial steps would come later, but the designers already understood that the ability to change the wing's shape at any given place made it vastly superior to a traditional sail.

Scott Ferguson, a Newport-based naval architect who was the wing's lead designer, told the group he wanted to alter the shape of the lowest section of the wing to make it more bowed because the increased curvature would enable it to capture more energy from the wind. Because increased force on the bottom of the wing wouldn't tip the boat as much as the same force higher up, the wing would be able to deliver more thrust before the boat heeled over too far.

The advantages were obvious. So to were the dangers. The wing was larger than a 747's wing, but it weighed just 2,811 pounds. In designing it, Ferguson had walked a delicate line, balancing the need for strength against the performance-enhancing benefits of lightness. The safety margins were small. By Ferguson's own standards, the boat was already overpowered—wound so tight, as it were, that one wrong move could cause it to snap. The sixteen sensors he had set up to track movements and loads on various components of the wing had set off alarms in every race.

But risks and rewards were being weighed differently now. Prior to the start of racing, even minor changes to the wing would have been analyzed through extensive rounds of computer modeling and on-the-water testing. Now, thanks to the scoreboard, the decision-making process was entirely different. Coutts and Simmer approved Ferguson's plan almost immediately.

But later on, Ferguson decided to hold off on implementing his change. When he heard Ainslie was joining the crew, he reasoned that it would be a mistake to introduce two major changes in the same race.

The cheating scandal had complicated the situation: one of the Oracle crew members who had been banned from sailing for the Cup, a penalty that was imposed just a few days before the first race, was Dirk de Ridder, a Dutch sailor who had always been the person who adjusted—in sailor speak, trimmed—the wing's position for Spithill. He was found to have been involved in illegally adding weight to a strut near the bow of the forty-five-foot catamaran that Oracle sailed against the challenger teams in a series of races that took place during 2011 and 2012 at various locations around the world. Adding the weight, which may have improved the boat's performance, violated rules that required that the boats used by each of the teams be identical to one another in every respect.

Eliminating de Ridder from the team was a huge penalty, potentially even more significant than the imposition of the two negative points, because sailing the AC72s optimally required keeping the position and angles of the wings and hydrofoils in perfect balance with the speed and direction of the wind, and that could only be achieved with meticulous coordination between the trimmer and helmsman. De Ridder and Spithill had performed the same roles not just during the races on the forty-five-footers and weeks of training with the AC72s but also during the America's Cup races in 2010. The thousands of hours of shared experience could not be replicated.

"You get to the point that you know what the other guy is thinking," Spithill told me. "That's something you can't shortcut."

De Ridder was replaced by Kyle Langford, a twenty-four-year-old Australian who was also found to have had a role in adding the illegal weight but was only given a warning. Langford, who became the youngest member of the sailing team, had trimmed the wing for Spithill for just a few days.

While the design team met, the sailors were studying data about the relative performance of the teams during each leg of the first five races. From the outset it had been clear that the Kiwi boat was significantly faster than

Oracle going upwind. When the Kiwi boat tacked, its "bottom speed"—that is, the speed to which it slowed as it turned through the eye of the wind—was typically about twelve knots. Oracle lost significantly more velocity, generally bottoming out at around eight knots. As a result, Oracle lost at least fifty feet on the competition every time both boats tacked.

*When a hull rose from the water, the AC72 accelerated rapidly.*

And while New Zealand's AC72 didn't lift completely out of the water during the upwind leg, a substantial portion of each its hulls did, allowing them to skim across the water. With less water resistance, the Kiwi moved faster. For Oracle, the combined impact of these differences was devastating. Each race began with a short leg during which boats "reached," meaning the wind came from the side, followed by a downwind leg, then the upwind leg, then the second downwind sprint, and finally a short reach to the finish line. Oracle's boat appeared to have a slightly better pace going downwind, but even if it was the first to cross the starting line and did better during the two downwind legs, the Kiwis could go so much faster in the single upwind leg that they would end up in front.

\* \* \* \*

When racing resumed on Thursday, Ainslie was now the tactician, but the wing had not been modified because of Ferguson's unilateral decision to hold off.

Oracle was first to cross the starting line after it out-maneuvered New Zealand in the complicated battle of wits that precedes every start as each helmsman fights to put his boat in the most favorable position relative to the starting line, the wind direction, and the other vessel. Oracle maintained its leading during the first two legs of the race, but still lost, by forty-six seconds, because of its inferior upwind speed. The second race of the day was even worse. After the Kiwis built up a 275-meter advantage, the chatter on their boat suggested that they had settled into a reliable race-winning routine.

Dean Barker, the Kiwi skipper, at one point said to Ray Davies, his tactician, "Just keep going, right?" After Davies agreed, Barker's tone was workmanlike: "Let's just keep it simple."

\* \* \* \*

Barker, a deeply tanned forty-one year old, was leading a team from a small nation that had long punched far above its weight in athletic competition, particularly sailing. It's often said that no country has more boats relative to the size of its population, and it's a society in which almost every child builds and sails a dinghy. What's more, New Zealand's geographic isolation seems to have produced an odds-defying culture of scrappy persistence. Unlike all of the other leading contenders for the Cup, Team New Zealand has never had a single super-rich backer. And yet it had defeated an array of other challengers to sail in four out of the last five America's Cup competitions.

Russell Coutts, who won his first sailboat race when he was seven and his Olympic gold medal at twenty-two, played a major role in that story. He was at the helm when the Kiwis defeated American sailing legend Dennis Conner in five straight races to win the Cup in 1995. In 2000, he led the first successful defense of the Cup by a non-American team by winning four straight against an Italian team backed by Patrizio Bertelli, the chief executive and owner of fashion giant Prada. Barker, who was then twenty-eight, was the backup helmsman and Coutts stepped off the boat and let his protégé have the helm for the final race.

After that regatta, Coutts and much of his team was hired away by Swiss challenger Ernesto Bertarelli, the heir to a vast pharmaceutical fortune. In the 2003 Cup, Coutts ended up sailing for Bertarelli against Barker, who stayed with Team New Zealand and became its lead helmsmen. Both squads were dominated by Kiwis, but once again, Coutts's team won five straight races, giving him his fourteen America's Cup victories. Afterwards, Coutts and a core group of fellow Kiwis once again switched loyalties when they were hired by Larry Ellison. Team Coutts prevailed once again in the 2010 Cup regatta, though this time he was the team's CEO and not a member of the sailing squad. Jimmy Spithill was the helmsman.

\* \* \* \*

Once Dean Barker crossed the finish line in Thursday afternoon's race, the score was 6 to minus 1. The Kiwis needed only three more wins to take the Cup. Oracle needed ten.

Somehow the numbers did not seem to register with Spithill. In what seemed like an audacious assault on the reality of things, he continued to insist that Oracle would win during the press conference that followed every day of racing. He even spoke of the special satisfaction that would come from doing so after being in a very deep hole: "I think the question is, imagine if these guys lost from here—what an upset that would be. I mean, they've almost got it in the bag. So that's my motivation. That'd be one hell of a story."

# "Beast Mode"

Friday, September 13, was a scheduled non-race day, but Philippe Presti, the sailing coach, would later call it the single most important day of the regatta. He had become convinced that Oracle could not win races unless the team learned how to get its AC72 completely up on its foils during the upwind leg—in essence, doing what the Kiwis were doing, and then going one better.

At the start of the regatta, it was widely assumed that full-fledged foiling would occur only when the AC72s went downwind or across the breeze. It wasn't that they couldn't foil when going upwind. The problem was that it took too long to reach the speed required to foil, particularly when the breeze was light. To achieve the necessary momentum, Spithill generally had to bear away from the optimum course by steering away from the source of the wind by an extra twenty degrees. With the relatively short and narrow racecourse, it seemed more efficient to sail a slower but more direct course.

But now Presti had a new idea.

Normally, when a boat tacks, the person trimming the sail brings the sail (or wing) in to the point where he believes it will provide the greatest possible thrust in a single movement. Smaller adjustments are made continuously, but there is only one major move. Presti wanted to do something fundamentally different. After every tack, he wanted the crew to reel in the wing to the optimum position, then let it out, and then reel it in again. Repeatedly. Over and over. The faster the better.

Called "pumping," it is the same technique used by speed-seeking wind surfers—and, for that matter, by a duck flapping its wings as it struggles to take off from a lake.

Pumping is prohibited under the Racing Rules of Sailing, the international standard for sailboat racing, because the wind pressure and propulsion it creates are deemed to be "artificial." The concept underlying the rule is that propulsion can only come from the boat's interaction with wind and water—not from energy created by repetitious actions by the crew.

The 2013 America's Cup had its own set of rules, but it was based on the Racing Rules of Sailing. The two documents are so similar that many of the rules shared the same number, and in both documents pumping is prohibited under Rule 42. The language in the two documents is also almost identical; the only differences are related to the fact that the AC72s had wings and "daggerboards," the hydrofoils that were lowered through the center of each of the hulls when it was time to foil.

This is what the America's Cup version of Rule 42 says: "A yacht shall compete only by using the wind and water to increase, maintain or decrease its speed. Her crew may adjust the trim of the wing, sails, rudders and daggerboards and perform other acts of seamanship." Rules experts say the permissible adjustments to the wing did not include the repetitive movements that were required for pumping.

The Racing Rules of Sailing also includes a more explicit prohibition against pumping. Its Rule 42.2 lists a number of illegal techniques, including: "pumping: repeated fanning of any sail either by pulling in and releasing the sail." The America's Cup rules did not include this language. While this difference in the two sets of rules does not mean pumping was permitted in Cup races, the less explicit language may have led some Oracle team members to conclude that they had found a loophole.

\* \* \* \*

When I learned that Oracle had been systematically fanning the wing of its AC72, I asked several rules experts if pumping was allowed under the Cup's version of Rule 42. They told me it was not. Given that Oracle's pumping was not done in response to shifts in the direction of the wind, gusts or waves, they said repetitive pumping was a violation. However, when this book was originally published, the team's spokesman, Peter Rusch, argued otherwise. He said the fact that the word "pumping" was not included in the America's Cup version of Rule 42 meant it was permitted. In response to his assertion, I decided to do more research.

The men and women who determine whether rules have been violated in important sailing regattas are "International Judges," officials who are certified by World Sailing, the sport's international governing body. Once a race is completed, the Judges examine reports and evidence of possible rule breaking, and determine whether there were actual violations. The other officials who regulate races are umpires, who are positioned on the water to watch for potential infractions. There are about twenty International Judges in the United States, and I attempted to question each of them. In doing so, I pointed out the differences between the standard version of Rule 42 and the America's Cup version. Then I described Peter Rusch's rationale and asked for their reactions. Many declined to comment because binding determinations about the legality of what happened during the 34th America's Cup could only have been made during the event and by the officials who oversaw it.

But several Judges confirmed what I had been told before. They said Oracle's pumping was not allowed under the America's Cup version of Rule 42 even though the term was not specifically cited. They said that if the umpires had seen the pumping, Oracle would have been penalized and forced to stop using the technique. *Not one of the Judges accepted Peter Rusch's argument that pumping was permitted.*

There was only one way pumping might have been legal given Rule 42: the lead umpire for the 34th Cup, Mike Martin, could have altered the rule by issuing an "interpretation" of its meaning before or during the regatta. But for this to happen, he would have had to have consulted with the teams and posted an interpretation on a publicly available online notice board. There was no such notice.

* * * *

The pumping itself was a massive challenge. The muscle could only come from the "grinders," the brawny sailors who pushed and pulled at pedestal-mounted handles to drive the winch Kyle Langford used to bring in the wing. Until now, only two grinders had been dedicated to powering the winch. From now on, there would be six. And rather than waiting until Langford told them to turn the handles, they would do so constantly, to ensure he had an always-ready source of power.

Meanwhile, on that same Friday, the wing itself was at last being transformed. Holding off on the planned modification, Scott Ferguson realized, had been a terrible mistake. With the now nearly hopeless score, it was obvious that the time had come to lay everything on the line.

Ferguson knew the team's new strategy for upwind sailing was based on pumping, and he understood, perhaps better than anyone, why pumping could be valuable: it was—assuming the technique could be mastered—a sure-fire means for transforming sailor muscle into boat speed. "This kind of repetitive movement

made it possible to get the boat moving faster and get it to lift onto the foils much faster," he told me. Ferguson also recognized that converting sailor muscle into boat speed was precisely what is prohibited by Rule 42, but he was being paid to optimize the power of the wing, not to enforce the rules.

The dangers of pumping went beyond potential penalties from the race officials. The combination of the wing adjustments and the pumping would put the wing under more stress than ever. Possibly too much. The pressure on the wing sheet—the line that connected the bottom corner of the wing to the winch—would become so great that the alarms would be going off all the time. Ferguson decided to simply disable them.

Langford, who sometimes relied on the alarms to let him know when he should limit the tension on the sheet, thought that was a terrible idea. "The alarms tell me where we are," he told Ferguson. He was particularly worried about a particular wing component—Control Arm #2, one of the devices that regulated its shape. Because Langford thought it was particularly vulnerable to additional pressure, he thought it should have its own stress-detecting sensor. Ferguson overruled him on all counts. He didn't want the crew to be distracted by any alarms and he planned to take most of the sensors off the boat to reduce weight. Now that the team was up against the wall, caution had become unaffordable. The AC72 was either going to hold together or it wasn't.

"We're kind of going into unknown territory," he told Langford. "But we don't have a choice."

\* \* \* \*

The next contest, Race 8, started poorly for Oracle. After Dean Barker and Ray Davies bested Spithill and Ainslie during the pre-start maneuvering, the Kiwi boat was first across the line. Oracle continued to trail behind for the first and second legs. But then, at the start of the three-mile upwind leg, heretofore Oracle's downfall, the grinders got down to business.

Oracle was pumping. After each tack, Spithill would start by steering his best course, which took him as close to the source of the wind as possible without losing too much speed. Then he turned slightly downwind to gain additional speed. At that point, he would say, "Let's get it up" on foils—and that's when the pumping commenced.

Even before Spithill made the call, the winch used to control the wing sheet was spinning. Several weeks after the race, Langford—who didn't realize pumping was prohibited—told me about the details of his technique. At the start of each cycle, he let three feet of the wing sheet slip through his hands to let the wing out by the same distance. Seconds later, he tightened his grip on the line until it locked onto the spinning winch. This enabled him to rapidly retrieve the line—and the wing—by the same amount. As soon as the wing returned to its original position, he again eased his grip to allow three feet of the line out. "As soon as I released it, I brought it back in," Langford explained. Let it out, reel it in, let it out, reel it in.

Each inward motion created additional air pressure against the wing, which immediately captured the resulting bursts of energy to give crucial boosts to the boat's velocity. When the breeze was relatively strong, Langford said it usually took five pumping actions to achieve foiling speed. In lighter breezes, additional cycles were required.

"The pumping was repeated, over and over, until the boat climbed up on the foils," remembers Rome Kirby, a twenty-four-year-old sailor from Newport, Rhode

Island, who was one of the grinders, and, now that Kostecki was gone, the crew's only American.

The pumping continued even after the AC72 was riding on its foils because the crew found that it could go faster and maintain a more advantageous course if they continued to flap the wing. "We had to keep it on the foil," Spithill told me. "It could only be done with aggressive pumping of the wing."

For the grinders, it was a cardiovascular marathon they called "beast mode." They were constantly engaged, whether the handles were revolving very fast, up to 100 revolutions per minute when there was little resistance, or twenty-five revolutions per minute when the wing was being pulled in. Most of the power came not from the grinders' arms but from their legs, making it a rhythmic, full-body exercise. The main limitation was aerobic capacity.

Joe Spooner, a thirty-nine-year-old from New Zealand—one of two Kiwis among the eleven-person crew that also included four Australians—was sailing in his fifth Cup regatta, but he was working much harder now than ever before. By the end of the race, Spooner, who is six foot four and weighs 225 pounds, had lost most of his feeling in his arms. A monitor indicated that his heart had been beating at more than 85 percent of its theoretical maximum rate of 181 throughout the race. In two short races, he would burn as many calories as he would have done running a marathon.

Everyone understood that the stresses on the wing

were approaching the breaking point. Ferguson originally thought the tension on the wing sheet would never be more than a ton. Now it regularly exceeded 1.6 tons.

But the pumping worked. After every turn, the frenzied in an out movements of the wing enabled the boat to rapidly climb up onto the foils. With the boat mostly liberated from the water's grip, Oracle quickly gained ground on the Kiwis. Thanks to the continued pumping, Spithill could then turn slightly back toward the source of the wind to put the boat on a more direct course toward the next mark without falling off the foils. Nonstop pumping was crucial. "If we didn't pump the wing, we would lose ground," Spithill explained. "I told the grinders, 'You're going to have beast mode all day.'"

"We're in the game!" Kirby shouted. "We're taking a ton out of them."

\* \* \* \*

Toward the end of the upwind leg, just when Oracle looked like it was in a position to take the lead, the Kiwis entered into a tack that went completely wrong. After they turned through the wind, their wing failed to alter its shape to adjust for the changed wind angle—it was curved in the wrong direction—and the inverted wing pushed the boat almost forty-five degrees beyond vertical, so far that it seemed certain to be on its way to capsizing. As it was upended, the boat also lost its forward momentum, and it suddenly looked like Oracle, still flying and heading toward the out-of-control vessel, would not have enough time to steer clear.

*Team New Zealand's AC72 seemed certain to capsize.*

As Spithill frantically pulled at the wheel to avert a double catastrophe, the Kiwis' boat continued to tip until it reached an absurd knife-edge equilibrium. There it hung for several seconds until, to the surprise of almost everyone, the runaway hull returned to the water with a crushing thud. Following an emergency tack, Oracle avoided a collision, seized the lead, and stormed toward the finish line.

The television commentators and journalists covering the Cup did not pick up on Oracle's pumping—they never would. Given the distances, the speed of the boats and the general rush of movements by the crew, the actions required to accomplish the pumping as well as the cycles of back and forth movements of the wing were imperceptible.

But everyone saw the result. While Oracle had to bear away from its optimal upwind course by twenty degrees in order to reach foiling speed before it developed its pumping technique, now it only had to bear away by half as much. And Oracle was improving on its pumping methodology in every race.

When it crossed the line, Oracle had earned its second win, which erased its final penalty point. It had clawed its way to zero. "What a momentum change," declared Kenny Read, a veteran sailor who was calling the race for NBC Sports. "If you're on Oracle right now, you have hope for the first time in many days."

# Match Point

No one forgot that Oracle was down by a score of 6 to 0, but Russell Coutts believed the team could stage a comeback if it continued to improve its upwind sailing. "I think your upwind mode could be even better," he told Spithill immediately after the race. And there were other improvements. Overnight, the wing was further modified. Once again, Ferguson increased the bow of the wing's lower sections, increasing the curvature by an increment equal to half of what was done in the previous alteration.

The changes appeared to be effective the next day. Oracle gained ground against the Kiwis in every leg of the first race and picked up another win. The second race of the day was a different story. Neither boat got very far ahead of the other and the lead changed four times, but New Zealand ended up winning the nail-biter of a contest by sixteen seconds.

Spectators in San Francisco and television audiences around the world were thrilled by the racing. Sailors who had criticized the AC72s were beginning to praise Ellison and Coutts for delivering on their promise to revolutionize the Cup. "If you didn't enjoy today's racing, you should probably watch another sport," Dean Barker said shortly after the race. Ben Ainslie agreed: "This is the most fun and exciting sailing I've been involved with."

But Oracle's position was dire. Its performance was continuing to improve—the team was at last holding its own—but the Kiwis were ahead by 7 to 1.

Again Oracle's engineers worked overnight. The bowsprit, the spar that extends forward from the ship's prow, was replaced with a smaller one to reduce weight and wind resistance, and the undersides of each of the hulls were slightly altered to give them a shape that engineers hoped would rise out of the water more easily.

Paul Bieker, a naval architect from Seattle who had designed everything from small sailing dinghies to high-speed ferries, focused on the hydrofoils. The foils did more than create lift. When the boat was completely up on its foils, they also counteracted the sideways push of the breeze. The force of the wind against the wing was substantial, now more so than ever, and that force was transferred to the much smaller foils. Indeed, the forces against the wing and the foils were not just opposite but also equal. This meant the foils, while not nearly as prominent to the eye as the wing, were enormously important.

The largest foils were the two retractable daggerboards. With shapes that resembled the curved outermost section of a modern airplane wing, the daggerboards, which were located halfway between the front and the back of the hulls, carried most of the boat's weight. The "rudder foils" were made from horizontal pieces of carbon fiber that were joined to the bottom of each of the rudders to create the shape of an inverted T.

*The daggerboard is retracted and the hull rides on its rudder foil.*

The design and fabrication of the foils had consumed more than 10,000 man-hours, but Bieker knew they were fundamentally flawed. Whenever the AC72's speed approached forty knots, the foils shook so violently that the entire vessel shuddered. It felt like airplane turbulence or, as Jimmy Spithill put it, "like driving over speed bumps at 100 miles per hour." In fact, the vibrations—the result of cavitation, a phenomenon common on very fast powerboats but virtually unheard of in relation to sailing vessels—had the same effect as speed bumps: they caused resistance that slowed the boat. The cavitation also impaired the foils' lifting capacity and allowed the rudders to slip sideways, giving Spithill a feeling similar to what happened when he made a sharp turn on a dirt bike and the back tire slid sideways.

Cavitation occurred because water passed each side of the foils at very different velocities, creating pressure differentials and vacuum-like force so great as to cause water to vaporize. San Francisco Bay was not even close to warm, but water was literally boiling, and the pockets of vapor that resulted became trapped next to the foils. From above, the vapor bubbles looked like harmless little clouds of milky white, but the foils' interaction with the gaseous spaces is what caused the vibrations, the sideways slipping, as well as speed-impairing resistance. Worse still, when the pockets collapsed, the water that filled the voids rushed at the foils so quickly that it tore off the orange paint and pocked the carbon surfaces. It looked as if someone had attacked them with an ice pick, and the rough surfaces slowed the boat even after the cavitation subsided.

The team's fluid dynamics experts believed eliminating the cavitation related to the rudder-foil would add at least four tenths of a knot to the boat's speed—or forty feet per minute, easily enough to change the outcome of a close race.

Eradicating the cavitation of the much larger dagger-boards would be even more beneficial, but there wasn't nearly enough time to design and build a new set of those, so Bieker focused on the rudder-foils. After experimenting with several ideas, he designed a fixture that could be installed at the place where the rudder was joined to the foil. There would be two components: a cone-like form that could go in front and a tapered fin that would go behind. There was no time for analysis and testing, so, like Ferguson, Bieker's design was based on his experience and intuition. His guiding thought was that he should give the rudder-foils a shape that mimicked those of the cavitation bubbles, which he hoped would balance the flow of water to diminish the pressure differentials.

Following Race 10, the one that took the score to 7-1, Bieker and a team of five boat builders, two Americans and three Kiwis, laminated the new fixture into place. Then they slathered on an epoxy-based compound and sculpted the result to give it a look Bieker judged to be aerodynamic, cured it inside heat tents, and smoothed the surfaces with sandpaper. They then added more epoxy and repeated the sculpting, baking, and sanding processes three more times. It took all night—they finished at 6 a.m., just before the arrival of the "measurers," race officials who inspected the boat before and after every race to search for evidence of race-rule violations.

But a few hours later, Oracle lost again after another close battle, bringing the score to 8 to 1. Match point. After the AC72 returned to base and was pulled out of the water, Bieker was thrilled to see that the paint on the altered rudder-foils was entirely unblemished. He was happier still when Spithill told him that the AC72 didn't feel like it was slipping sideways anymore. "I didn't lose grip," the skipper said.

But the larger story was now impossibly bleak. New Zealand needed just one more win to secure the Cup. Oracle needed to win eight in a row. For Oracle, death could come at any moment.

# There Are No Shortcuts

If the Kiwis felt good about their prospects, they didn't let it show. "We're obviously very happy to sneak away with another win," Dean Barker told a reporter immediately after the race. But as his choice of words suggested, there was no triumphalism. Indeed, moments later, at the daily press conference, he acknowledged the improved performance of Oracle's AC72, saying, "The boats have just come together in terms of performance." Ray Davies, the Kiwi tactician, made it clear that they were taking nothing for granted. "We've got to sail every race as best we can and push the boat really, really hard," he said. "As soon as you back off a little bit on these boats, your lead can get chopped down really quick."

In the face of the impossible odds, Oracle's leadership did what it could to maintain the crew's morale. Larry Ellison, making a rare appearance at the team's base, spoke individually to the sailors. So did Presti, who emphasized the need to think not about winning or losing the Cup but making the best possible effort, one race at a time.

"It's looking bloody tough," Coutts acknowledged during an all-team meeting, "but we're sailing really well." He also tried to put an improved spin on things by citing an aspect of America's Cup history: "Most Cup regattas are decided in a whitewash—one team wins all the races." Everyone knew that's exactly what happened when Coutts was at the helm in 1995, 2000, and 2003. "We now have the better package," he continued, "so there's no reason we can't win the next eight races. We just have to make sure we don't make any mistakes."

But almost everyone, Coutts included, knew that scenario was extraordinarily unlikely. With a single exception, every member of the sailing squad told me they had by then concluded that winning had become an unrealistic aspiration. They would continue to give it their all, because that's what they always did, but it was mostly about saving face.

The exception was Jimmy Spithill. When he arrived at his Marina District apartment a few hours after the defeat that landed him on match point, his American wife Jennifer was obviously upset. With tears falling down her cheeks, she kept saying the same thing, over and over. "I'm sorry. I'm so sorry." Spithill told her to stop. "We're going to win," he declared. "There's a long way to go, but we're going to do it." Later on, Spithill told me he really believed that, even then.

\* \* \* \*

It is difficult to imagine how anyone could be more competitive than Jimmy Spithill. Growing up in a small community north of Sydney that can only be reached by boat, he declared his America's Cup ambitions at age nine. At twenty, he became the youngest skipper in Cup history when he was given the helm for an Australia-sponsored team in 1999. In 2010, he became the youngest winning helmsman in the history of the Cup. Spithill played almost every sport you can think of—not just those involving water but also golf, tennis, and basketball, to name a few—and he was forever eager to turn everyday aspects of life into contests. No matter what it was, he fought to win as if his life were on the line.

*Jimmy Spithill*

Fighting itself—boxing—was one of his other favorite sports, and Oracle employed a boxing coach as part of its physical-fitness program because Spithill believed it provided ideal training for AC72s.

"If you make a mistake in the ring, it's obvious what's going to happen. It's the same on this boat. When you make a mistake on this boat, you also really get punished," he explained. "And when you're boxing, you have to make decisions when you're totally exhausted. Same on the boat. Thinking is usually the first thing that goes when you're tired, and boxing teaches you about discipline. There are no shortcuts."

\* \* \* \*

On September 19, Oracle bounced back to win Race 12. But the next day, when the wind was unusually light by San Francisco's blustery standards, it looked as if Oracle's final hour had well and truly come. The alterations to the wing, which had proven to be a major plus when the wind was strong, became a negative when conditions were lighter, and the team made several minor but consequential mistakes. Team New Zealand sailed a near-perfect race to amass a mile-long lead, and the mood on the Oracle boat was terrible.

It was even worse on the team's chase boats. "How could they throw it away like this?" Grant Simmer demanded. Coutts had reverted to tirade mode, a non-stop profanity-fueled rant that ceased only when Ian Burns, who was responsible for collecting and analyzing performance data for the team but was then driving the boat, pointed out that New Zealand was unlikely to make it to the finish line within the forty-minute time limit. A rule devised to facilitate television coverage meant this race probably wouldn't count.

The sailors didn't know that. Even in light breeze, there was always such a frenzy of rushed activity that they were almost completely oblivious to time. Spithill did think about the time limit at one point, but when he glanced at his watch, he only became confused because he had forgotten that the start of the race had been delayed. When he finally heard that the race had been abandoned, he gulped down a big breath and said, "Okay boys, we've been given another life." The sailors were of course relieved, but having been convinced that it was all over, they were also emotionally empty. For Joe Spooner, it was the worst moment of the entire regatta.

"We had made so many mistakes and we thought we had lost the America's Cup," he said. "And now we had to sail another race in thirty minutes."

When one of the chase boats approached the AC72 shortly after the race was aborted, Spithill waved it off. "We're going to need a few minutes on our own," he said over the radio. As the crew gathered around him, he said, "Let's talk about what went wrong." Remarkably, in spite of all the disappointments and the private doubts, the team's morale had remained strong and there had never been even a hint of second-guessing or finger pointing. Now, one by one, the crewmen owned up to mistakes and talked about what would happen next time. Almost everyone had something to say. When they were done, Spithill said, "OK guys, let's get on with it."

The breeze was stronger for the restarted race and New Zealand took an early lead, but Oracle, benefiting from a favorable shift in the wind direction, won by a substantial margin.

After the race, Spithill hit on a brazen new approach for putting a positive slant on the standings, claiming that the team was actually benefitting from the stress of being so far behind: "The fact that we are at match point—we get the best out of our people when they're at that sort of pressure. We take it one at a time."

# Looking for Wind

Two days after the near-death experience, on September 22, bold tactical decisions were again on center stage during another day of light and patchy wind.

In most races, the tactician on the leading boat seeks to position his vessel in between his opponent and the next mark to make it difficult for the other boat to get ahead by capitalizing on more favorable wind or current in a different section of the racecourse. If the second boat heads off to one side of the racecourse, the lead boat also moves to that side. So if a stronger breeze develops in that section of the racecourse or if there's an advantageous change in the direction of the wind, both boats are likely to benefit in equal measure. But in the day's first contest, Race 14, Ainslie decided to abandon the normal approach, focusing on directing Spithill to areas where he believed the wind was strongest without regard for what the Kiwi's were doing. This could open up potentially race-winning opportunities to the Kiwis—but it could be decisive if Ainslie, by studying the surface of the water, flags, and any other indicators of wind strength, was able to determine where the breeze was best.

The stratagem worked and Oracle won, bringing the score to 8-4. The second race of the day was another light-air battle of wits, and Oracle prevailed again after Ainslie made a series of flawless judgments on the wind.

On September 23, a day with a much steadier breeze, Ainslie's tactical calls were again consistently on target. Equally important, Oracle's wing was pumping with eagle-like might, making it possible for the team to repeatedly climb up on the foils faster than the Kiwis. The team had continued to hone its pumping methodology to the point that now it would mount the foils during the upwind leg by bearing away from its desired course by only five degrees.

With five straight wins, the score was now 8-6. If Oracle hadn't been hit with the two-point penalty, the score would be tied, a fact Spithill called "motivating" when he spoke to reporters after the race. More importantly, the sense that a Kiwi victory was inevitable had given way to a wholly different reality: it seemed as if the Kiwis *could not win*. They just couldn't close the deal.

The change in fortune was obviously weighing on Dean Barker. The soft-spoken helmsman never seemed to enjoy the verbal jousting that took place at the post-race press conferences—not even when he was sitting on a commanding lead—but now he looked forlorn, even pained. Spithill, who regarded journalistic engagements as just another form of combat, seized on Barker's weakness. With the starchy confidence of an army general, he declared, "We really have a huge wave of momentum right now." Implying that there had been another round of boat improvements, he went on to say, "Again last night the shore team was there to the early hours of the morning."

*Jimmy Spithill used press conferences to put additional pressure on Dean Barker.*

In fact, there had been no significant changes to the boat that night, which Spithill was happy to acknowledge when I spoke to him later. "I was just trying to wind Dean up," he explained. "If I can get into his head and rattle him, I'll do it. I will do whatever it takes to help my team."

For all the bravado and gamesmanship, no one lost sight of the brutal reality: Oracle was still at match point. A single tactical error, botched maneuver, or breakage could end it all in a matter of minutes.

But everything else had changed. Most importantly, Oracle now appeared to have the faster boat, and the story of how that came to be carried with it momentum of its own, not to mention lessons with much broader applications: Oracle's reincarnation was born of not just never-say-die determination and unspoken prohibitions on finger pointing and naysaying but also of an almost reckless willingness to accept risk. The hopeless prospects had yielded a game-changing freedom to go for broke. Without that—and a willingness to ignore Rule 42—the team never would have learned how to get the most out of its boat.

Now it was the Kiwis who were on the back foot, and at this point there wasn't nearly enough time for them to undertake similar reinvention.

\* \* \* \*

No one outside the team was aware of Oracle's pumping methodology, but the fact that it had broken the rules on the forty-five-foot boat and the suddenly improved performance of its AC72 gave rise to rumors of other illegal practices. The most widely circulated story suggested that Oracle had installed a computerized "stability augmentation system" that automatically adjusted the positions of the hydrofoils to keep the boat flying and perfectly level above the water. The allegation had just enough specifics to sound credible: Oracle's system was allegedly based on the same technology Boeing 747s use to control the flaps on their wings. Oracle's secret weapon was even said to have a nickname—"Herbie." Such a system would violate rules that prohibit any adjustments to the foils (or the wing) that are not instigated by the crew itself.

But there was no Herbie. A stability augmentation system would have required sensors and an onboard computing device, and the boat was rigorously inspected before and after every race by the measurers, who were on the lookout for physical evidence of any violations. They found none.

\* \* \* \*

September 24 was another big day for Oracle and also for Ellison, who was supposed to deliver a keynote speech to the 60,000 people who had come to San Francisco for Oracle Corporation's biggest customer event of the year. Ellison skipped his speech and, it turned out, he would not be disappointed by the sailing.

The first race began when Barker, struggling to improve his position near the starting line, allowed his boat to make contact with Oracle's, which resulted in a pair of penalties that meant the Kiwi boat had to stop sailing for several seconds. New Zealand never recovered, and Oracle chalked up its sixth straight win. After the race, Barker acknowledged what was becoming obvious to everyone: Oracle's AC72 had become the faster boat. The outcome of most America's Cup regattas is ultimately determined by the relative speeds of the boats and it looked like Oracle had the edge.

"It's clear to see they were going pretty damn well," Barker said. "It was the first time that we recognized there was a condition where maybe we aren't as strong as we need to be."

In the second race, New Zealand got the better start and it maintained a slight lead throughout the downwind leg. During the upwind leg, Oracle, pumping furiously, climbed up on its foils before the Kiwis and pulled ahead. It gained additional margin with every tack and soon built an unassailable lead. In the end, Oracle crossed the finish line almost a full minute ahead of the Kiwis to win its seventh straight race.

Remarkably, three weeks after the start of racing, the series stood at an 8-8 tie. For the first time in thirty years, the America's Cup would be decided by a sudden-death finish.

# "We Have a Problem"

Forty-five minutes before the start of the final race, Oracle was sailing upwind when Kyle Langford looked aloft and noticed a small bulge in the wing about thirty feet from the bottom. It was, he immediately realized, the location of Control Arm #2, the device he had worried about when Scott Ferguson started making his adjustments to the wing.

"Jimmy, let's jump over—something doesn't look right," he shouted to Spithill, wanting him to turn the boat so the wing would swing from one side to the other. When it did, Langford could see a similar bulge projecting from the same place on the opposite side of the wing. Now Langford was really worried. "Jimmy, we have to stop! We have a problem."

Within minutes, Ferguson, who was onboard one of the team's chase boats, was on the AC72 along with Jeff Causey, the wing's main rigger, who put on a harness so he could be hoisted up to see the problem.

Ascending the wing was much more difficult than climbing the mast of a traditional sailboat because there wasn't much to hold onto and everything was so delicate. One false move and a hand or foot could puncture the plastic film. Knowing this and also that the race could not be delayed because Oracle had already played its single postponement card, the passengers on Russell Coutts' boat were horrified to see a spider-man-like figure dangling next to the wing just minutes before the scheduled start of the final race.

Ian Burns, who was again at the wheel of Coutts' boat, tapped out a text message to his wife, Oracle Corporation's chief marketing officer Judith Sim, who was with Ellison on his boat.

"Problem with the wing," Burns wrote.

Sim's reply was instantaneous: "Should I tell Larry?"

Burns said "not yet," but then the urgency of things soon became obvious when Spithill spoke over the radio: "We need boat builders and all the super-fast-drying glue we can get. Right now!"

Hearing this, Ellison called Coutts, who was unable to offer much in the way of encouragement. "One of the control arms is damaged," Coutts reported. "The guys are trying to fix it."

Reaching the bulge, Causey used a penknife to slice through the plastic film so he could peel back a section and see what was wrong. The control arm itself appeared to be undamaged, but the bracket that was supposed to hold it in place had broken. If the control arm became completely unfastened, which seemed inevitable with the stress of more sailing, the wing would be unable to change its shape as it was moved from side to side. Racing would be hopeless. Returning to the deck, Causey described the damage to Ferguson and Langford.

"The best we can do," he said, "is make some more brackets and stick them in with as much glue as we can."

Langford believed the problem was probably incurable, but rather than tell the other sailors that he said the opposite: "Don't worry, it will be fine. Jeff just needs to glue it back together."

Minutes later, the sailors' anxiety intensified when they heard the whine of a battery-powered circular saw. Dan Smith, one of several boat builders who had come onboard, was cutting strips of carbon fiber into L-shaped pieces of various sizes that would hopefully serve as brackets. Causey was already back up on the wing with a glue gun. As soon as the makeshift brackets were lifted to him, he pumped glue onto the side of the control arm and positioned four of the brackets. Then he used his hands to layer in more glue.

Spectators and journalists were unaware of Oracle's crisis, but Scott Ferguson was on the verge of panic. The thought that the epic comeback might derail now because of the failure of the wing—his wing—was hard to take. Not being able to see exactly what had gone wrong or do anything to help made it even worse. He was already thinking about the impact this might have on his career and how he might try to explain himself. "We lived by the sword and we died by the sword," he ended up saying to himself. When Causey came down, he worried that the glue wouldn't cure before the start of the race, but he put the odds of a successful repair at 80 percent.

Langford asked, "Do we need to take it easy?"

What would be the point of that, Causey said to himself. It was the decisive race. The boat would hold together or it wouldn't. "No," he told Langford. "If you're comfortably ahead, cruise it, but otherwise, go hard." Then, thinking again about how the lack of a functioning control arm would make it impossible to move the wing, he recalibrated: "If you can see an obvious problem, minimize your maneuvers."

That's where the conversation ended because Spithill was shouting at the non-sailors. "You have to get off the boat!"

\* \* \* \*

When the final race began, New Zealand took an early lead. Russell Coutts didn't raise his voice. He didn't say anything. His level of stress had become so great that he could not bring himself to even watch—not even during the upwind sprint, when the teams engaged in the most exciting tacking duel of the entire regatta. "Watching these races is much harder than being in them," Coutts told me afterwards. "It was horrible."

Even with the make-or-break pressure, both crews sailed flawlessly. But for Oracle, two weeks of refinements came together with unified intensity. The grinders whirred their handles, working harder than ever as Langford pumped the wing after every tack.

"This is it—this is it," Ainslie shouted at one point. "Work your asses off!"

Oracle took the lead during the upwind leg, then lost it, then took it back again. Both boats were flying across the bay, but Coutts didn't see any of it. He was just staring at the floor of the boat and waiting for the sailing to end. At the conclusion of the upwind battle, Oracle had the lead. During the final downwind leg, both boats flew at better than forty-five miles per hour, and Oracle expanded its advantage. As it closed in on the finish line, spectators on a nearby pier erupted in cheers and raised their arms to wave American flags and capture the moment by taking photos with their phones.

*Both crews sail flawlessly.*

Crossing the line, the sailors also raised their arms. Some of them clenched their fists. They had pulled off the unthinkable, the biggest comeback in America's Cup history, perhaps the greatest comeback in all of sport. But even as they screamed and embraced one another, their emotions were more complicated than mere elation, the feeling of relief almost as great as the euphoria. This was also true for Scott Ferguson. Although he had never been much for hugging, he found himself in a tearful embrace with Jeff Causey. Paul Bieker was surprised to find that he was both elated and sad, already feeling a sense of loss because there would be no more races. "Wars are probably the only other time when you get this kind of focus and teamwork, and now it was over," he explained.

Joe Spooner was totally spent. "The incredible thing is that we didn't implode," he told me afterwards." It would have been so easy for the team to start criticizing each other, and then it would have all fallen apart."

There was also a palpable sense of disbelief. Because everyone had been so focused on making the next step rather than reaching a mountaintop that had for so long seemed impossible, the recognition that they had succeeded was slow to gel. Larry Ellison sensed that. After he climbed onboard the AC72, he kept asking a question that otherwise would have sounded absurdly clueless: "Do you know what you've done? You've won the America's Cup!"

There would be plenty of time to savor the victory, but it would have to wait, at least momentarily. Jimmy Spithill steered the boat away from the cheering crowds to foil once more—this time just for Ellison. Remarkably, the man who had spent more than $200 million to retain the Cup had never even set foot on the boat before. Now, as he struggled to maintain his balance, Team Oracle headed out into the bay. This time there was no need to pump the wing, but once again, the boat picked up speed, and as it did it rose above the water and picked up more. As the speed reached its maximum, Ellison, for the first and only time, took the wheel.

# Afterword

At a crowded press conference a couple of hours later, some of the assembled journalists clearly believed Oracle's comeback resulted from something singular, not just the accumulated benefits of various marginal enhancements. "You mentioned that you broke the code," Joe Vasquez, a reporter for KPIX, the CBS television affiliate in San Francisco, said to Ellison. "A lot of people want to know: what do you mean that you broke the code?"

Smiling, Ellison replied, "Is Russell in the room? Are we allowed to talk about that? Or is it going to be a big secret?" Russell Coutts was not on the dais and he declined to speak up from the back of the room, so Ellison continued. He acknowledged that the crew had hit on a powerful new technique, but he would not describe it. "The boys sailed the boat quite a bit differently," he said. "We increased the horsepower of the boat. I guess I'm not going to go into details of exactly what we did."

A few minutes later, Tom Fitzgerald, a reporter for the *San Francisco Chronicle,* put the same question to Jimmy Spithill: "Since Larry is not going to be more forthcoming about how you got the extra horsepower, can you tell us exactly how you did it?"

Spithill tried to deflect the question with a joke: "I was just winding you guys up. We didn't change a thing."

The room erupted in laughter, but Fitzgerald persisted, and Spithill eventually said, "There are so many changes we made. There were physical changes to the boat. There were a lot of technique changes like Larry alluded to." He wouldn't say anything more.

\* \* \* \*

During the months that followed, rumors about Oracle's methods continued to swirl, and then another important question arose: where would the next competition for the Cup take place?

Given that San Francisco was Ellison's home base and that the final races had attracted a lot of attention, it was widely assumed that the competition would remain there. But insiders knew that Oracle's relationship with the city was fraught. During the negotiations that preceded the 2013 regatta, Coutts and Ellison had demanded a host of economic benefits from the city. They didn't get everything they asked for, but many civic leaders believed the city had granted an unseemly subsidy to California's richest man. According to various reports, the Cup ended up costing taxpayers millions of dollars and anticipated new employment had failed to materialize.

Coutts didn't rule San Francisco out, but he said he and Ellison were also exploring several other possibilities: San Diego, Newport, Chicago, and Hawaii. There was a logic for each of them, particularly for Ellison. San Diego and Newport had both been the venue for multiple America's Cup regattas. Ellison owned a grand house in Newport, the onetime summer estate of the Astor family, and he grew up in Chicago. He also had a major foothold in Hawaii, having spent $300 million to acquire almost the entire island of Lanai. For a time, Hawaii appeared to be the leading contender, but then the list was expanded to include a location that wasn't even in the United States—Bermuda. Given that the America's Cup had been established as a "friendly competition between foreign nations," this last possibility came as a major surprise.

For most of the Cup's history, nationality was its central theme. Sailors always came from their campaign's country of origin, and so did the designers and builders of their boats and the makers of its sails. Over the years, nationality requirements had been loosened, but there was a growing sense that Oracle was pushing too far. To most U.S. sailors, the fact there was just one American on board Oracle's AC72 during the final races in 2013 seemed absurd.

Selecting a foreign venue would not be entirely unprecedented. After Ernesto Bertarelli, the Swiss billionaire, won the Cup in 2003, he selected Valencia, Spain as the venue for 2007, but because Switzerland is a landlocked nation his options were limited.  For a winning team with several viable domestic alternatives to chose a foreign venue would be an entirely different matter. For many America's Cup fans, it was almost beyond comprehension.

But Ellison went with the unthinkable, announcing that the 35th America's Cup would be held in a British overseas territory 600 miles from the east coast of the United States. The decision was largely based on economics. Bermuda's government agreed to subsidize the regatta—which was set for June 2017—with a financial package valued at $77 million. In addition, Coutts and Ellison hoped the island's mid-Atlantic location would encourage television distributors to offer live broadcasts in both the United States and Europe.

But the decision seemed sure to have non-financial costs. "The Cup was always about nationality—the Americans against the world or the Kiwis against the world," says John Rousmaniere, a noted author and sailor who has written about the event for decades. "That's the key to what made the America's Cup a special event. Now that that's gone, the Cup is becoming irrelevant."

Once again, the racing would be on high-speed, hydrofoiling catamarans, though they would be smaller than they had been in San Francisco (62 feet long rather than 72), part of an effort to reduce costs and attract more teams. Ellison predicted that a dozen teams would sign up for the 35th Cup, so many that he said the racing would be organized into Pacific and Atlantic divisions. In fact, including Oracle, there would be just six.

\* \* \* \*

After it became known that Oracle had pumped its wing to increase its boat speed in the 34th Cup, it was inevitable that the other teams would attempt to develop similar techniques for the racing in Bermuda and also in preliminary races that were scheduled for Oman, New York, Chicago, Portsmouth (England), and Toulon (France).

But the circumstances would be different from what they were in San Francisco: now it was widely understood that wing-pumping was technically possible, there was no chance that it would go unnoticed by the officials, and multiple teams wanted to do it. And so, after discussions between the teams and the umpire who officiate in 2017, Richard Slater, it was determined that pumping would be allowed in the 35th Cup. On March 11, 2016, Slater announced the new approach on the notice board, declaring that the teams "may pull in and release the wing or any other sail without restriction."

Slater's decision did not retroactively make Oracle's pumping during the 34th America's Cup legal—that could only have been done by the umpire for that event, and he would have to have publicly announced that he was doing so before or during the 2013 regatta—but

Slater's announcement would be profoundly important to the racing in the 35th America's Cup. A long-banned technique would become a legitimate part of the game in sailing's best-known contest. Oracle's technique would go from being a secret weapon to a central, perhaps even decisive component of the competition.

It also seemed likely that the new approach would put further distance between the America's Cup and the rest of sailing. By making the boats faster and, most particularly, enabling them to get up on their foils more rapidly, universal pumping was likely to advance Ellison's goal of turning the Cup into a television-ready, big-time global sporting event. But that's not what most sailors want the Cup to become, particularly if it requires sacrificing what they regard as a fundamental principle. They believe sailing is about using traditional seamanship to manage the interactions between boat, wind and water. Systems designed to turn sailor brawn into propulsion are, for them, an abomination.

*Scuttlebutt Sailing News,* a popular daily newsletter for competitive sailors around the world, broke the news that pumping would be permitted in the 2017 edition of the America's Cup. One day later, By Baldridge, a onetime Cup sailor and a former commodore of the Houston Yacht Club, contributed a comment to the newsletter that captured a widespread view of what legalized pumping would mean for the America's Cup. "It seems to me," he wrote, "that this is no longer a sailing competition."

# Sailing Stories

*T*he *Wall Street Journal* I joined in 1994 didn't have a sports page and it didn't cover sailing. What it did have was Leisure & Arts, the creation of Ray Sokolov, a gifted editor who seemed to be interested in pretty much everything. During the summer of 1999, not long after I had become the *Journal*'s Hong Kong correspondent, I asked Ray if he would publish my first-person account of a race across the South China Sea. He said yes, and, once I filed my report, he made it clear that he wanted more sailing stories. A year later, I was in Auckland writing about the America's Cup.

By then, Ray had named me the *Journal*'s "yachting correspondent." It wasn't really a job. There wouldn't be many assignments or much in the way of extra pay. But the fringe benefits were enormous, starting with the writers with whom I shared the page, which included Pulitzer Prize winners Ada Louise Huxtable, the architecture critic, and Manuela Hoelterhoff, who wrote about theatre and opera. The yachting correspondent wouldn't win any journalistic prizes, but I received lots of irresistible invitations—to go to regattas, to review books, to even sail across oceans.

What follows are ten of my favorite sailing stories, arranged chronologically. All but two were published in the *Journal*. Some are about my own adventures, but I've also included book reviews and tributes to legendary sailors and vessels. A number of the pieces relate to one another, some intimately. For example, in 2002, I reviewed a book about the storied transatlantic race that was organized by Kaiser Wilhelm II in 1905 to advance Germany's maritime ambitions. A three-masted American schooner called *Atlantic* ended up spoiling the Kaiser's plans by winning the race—and it set a record that had stood ever since. In 2005, I was aboard *Mari-Cha IV*, the fastest single-hull sailboat the world had ever seen, when it entered another transatlantic race with the goal of breaking the century-old record.

When the 34th competition for the America's Cup began in San Francisco, I was off the coast of France sailing on *Spindrift 2*, a ridiculously fast trimaran that had circumnavigated the globe in just 45 days. When the crew let me take the helm, I got our speed up to 35.4 knots, or 41 miles an hour. It was an unforgettable thrill. It also helped me to understand what it was like to be Jimmy Spithill when he was at the wheel of Oracle's AC72.

# Race of Princes

*The Wall Street Journal*
*February 5, 2002*

The history of nautical extravagances is long and colorful. Egyptian pharaohs built luxurious yachts for cruising the Nile, an opulent vessel bore Cleopatra across the Mediterranean Sea to meet Mark Antony in 24 BC, and ancient Chinese rulers were obsessed with the idea of large floating palaces. Several of today's richest men are spending tens of millions of dollars to prepare for the next America's Cup, which takes place in New Zealand early next year.

But the most remarkable convergence of wealth and vessels occurred in the United States about a century ago. In 1900, before the imposition of income or inheritance taxes, members of the New York Yacht Club owned

47 yachts that were longer than 200 feet. Anthony Drexel's 352-foot schooner, sailed with a professional crew of 90, was almost as large as the U.S. Navy's biggest warships.

In 1905, eleven of the era's most impressive yachts gathered in New York Harbor for the start of the first major transatlantic race, which was sponsored by Kaiser Wilhelm II, the emperor of Germany, who promised to present the winner with a solid-gold cup. Outsized yachts have always been about more than just sailing, and as Scott Cookman writes in "Atlantic: The Last Great Race of Princes," the contest had everything to do with the Kaiser's headlong rush to turn Germany into an important sea power. Planning to enter his own yacht, which would be crewed by regulars from the German imperial navy, the Kaiser expected to award the cup to himself.

Two British aristocrats and eight super-rich Americans were determined to stop him.

Some of the best parts of Mr. Cookman's book are the portraits he paints of the competitors. We learn that the first man to take up the Kaiser's challenge was Lord Lindsay, the quirky 26th Earl of Crawford, who spent ten months of the year cruising around the world with his vast stamp collection on a 648-ton yacht that was outfitted with fireplaces, a grand piano and a formal dining room that could seat 30.

We also meet Wilson Marshall, the 36-year-old New York Yacht Club member who never worked a day in his life but who owned *Atlantic,* a three-masted schooner. Able to carry more than 20,000 square feet of sails, the 184-foot-long, steel-hulled vessel could power through the water at 20 knots even though it was weighed down by rooms that had marble floors and an opulently furnished grand saloon that was illuminated by three Tiffany skylights. Like most of the competitors, Marshall was onboard during the race, although he had no intention of helping out with the sailing. Accustomed as he was to ceaseless comfort and merriment, he and six guests would be served lavish meals by four liveried stewards, who also contributed nothing to the racing.

The race attracted far more press attention than contemporary yachting contests. Some of the coverage was critical, noting that the competition would be unfair because there weren't any limits on the size of the yachts or their crews. Lord Lindsay's craft was 245 feet long, more than double the 108-foot-long *Fleur de Lys.* Candace Stimson, the daughter of the *Fleur de Lys*'s owner (and sister of Henry L. Stimson the secretary of war during World War II), also received a lot of attention as the first woman to sail in a major ocean race.

Newspapers also covered the feverish efforts to recruit top-rated professional skippers. That was quite a happy story for the professionals: Seven of the American yacht owners agreed to pay their skippers at least $30,000, equal to more than a half-million of today's dollars, for an event that no one thought would take more than three weeks.

The race began off Sandy Hook, New Jersey, amid fog and rain and virtually no wind, but a few days later the fleet was swallowed up by the kind of violent storm that makes for the most exciting ocean races and, potentially, record-setting passages. Although the competitors didn't know it—only one had a radio—the race soon turned into a duel between *Hamburg,* the Kaiser's yacht, and *Atlantic,* which was skippered by Charlie Barr, the legendary yachtsman who had won three consecutive America's Cups.

Barr pushed *Atlantic* as hard as he could even though it was pitching so wildly that it was impossible for Marshall and his guests to enjoy the fine Champagne and vintage Bordeaux that had been brought onboard. It was worth it. *Atlantic* reached the Lizard, the headland that stands at Britain's southwestern-most point, 22 hours ahead of *Hamburg.* Having traveled at an average speed of 10.32 knots, *Atlantic* completed the crossing in 12 days, four hours and one minute, establishing a record sailors have been talking about ever since.

# *Mari-Cha IV* Sails Toward the Record Books

*The Wall Street Journal*
*May 26, 2005*

LATITUDE 40 30 NORTH, LONGITUDE 58 09 WEST—When we glided down the Hudson River and past the towers of midtown Manhattan, the start of the Rolex Transatlantic Challenge 2005 was still hours away. But adrenaline was already pumping. I was, after all, aboard *Mari-Cha IV,* the fastest single-hull sailboat the world has ever seen, and we were part of a remarkable fleet of yachts that would re-create the "Kaiser's Cup," a legendary transatlantic race that took place 100 years ago.

The starting line was off Sandy Hook, almost exactly the point from which 11 yachts had set out in the 1905 race. That contest came about after Kaiser Wilhelm II, the German emperor, challenged the biggest names in sailing to take part in what became the first international trans-atlantic race. While the Kaiser assumed that his yacht, *Hamburg*, would win, he wound up being defeated by a three-masted schooner called *Atlantic,* which was skippered by three-time America's Cup winner Charlie Barr. Having ridden a violent storm under full sail, *Atlantic* reached the English Channel in 12 days, four hours and one minute to establish the most storied record in yachting history. According to the sailing world's official record keeper, the World Sailing Speed Record Council, it is a record that still has not been broken.

Some of the 20 yachts in our field did not look very different from those that took part in the Kaiser's Cup. *Sumurun,* a stunningly beautiful 94-foot ketch with classic lines, immaculately varnished teak, and a soaring pair of Douglas fir masts, is almost old enough to have been there; it was launched in 1914. *Stad Amsterdam* is almost new, but the 257-foot square rigger looks like a vintage clipper ship. Some of the yachts in the 1905 race also functioned as floating palaces—the *Atlantic* made its mark in spite of being weighed down with marble floors, Tiffany skylights, four liveried stewards, and cases of wine—and it is no different in the current race. *Stad Amsterdam* has comfortable staterooms and three chefs. *Tiara,* a 178-foot-long sloop, has a duplex owner's suite and a fireplace. It is so big that a helicopter has landed on its stern deck, which is believed to be a first for a sailboat.

*Mari-Cha* is nothing like that. Except for the high-tech "nav station," where I am struggling to punch sensible words into a lurching keyboard, the rest of the 140-foot-long boat's interior is open and virtually unfurnished. Take my bunk: It is a "pipe berth," consisting of nylon mesh stretched over a rectangular frame of carbon-fiber pipes. And there are no liveried servants. Or wine. Our meals consist of freeze-dried food and granola bars.

Given the steady onslaught of wind and waves, the deck is a difficult place to be. Being below isn't much better, because of the motion of the vessel. It feels like we are on a plane stuck in a zone of endless turbulence. The noise level is also high—a mix of shrieking wind, rushing water, grinding winches, and explosion-like bangs every time the hull crashes off a wave.

This boat is devoted to one thing—speed—and there are virtually no compromises. With a pair of 140-foot masts and a 21-foot-long keel that can be hydraulically moved to one side or the other by up to 40 degrees to counteract the force of the wind, it can carry enormous sails and blast through the water at more than 30 knots (34.5 miles per hour). In 2003, it crossed the Atlantic in less than seven days, smashing the previous record by more than two days. Along the way, it sailed 525 miles in a 24-hour period, which was also a record for a single-hull sailboat.

Since that transatlantic record was not set as part of a scheduled race—*Mari-Cha*'s departure was timed to take advantage of favorable weather conditions—its record is in a different category than *America*'s.

The crew that ensures that the boat is always moving at its optimal speed is every bit as extraordinary as our craft. Bob Miller, the billionaire founder of Duty Free Shoppers, is our skipper and the man who paid for this gleaming thrill-making machine. We also have a "racing skipper" named Mike "Moose" Sanderson, who has competed in several America's Cup competitions and won the Whitbread Round the World Race, and a team of other top-rated professional sailors. In addition to me, there are four other amateurs: Mr. Miller's sons-in-law, Crown Prince Pavlos of Greece, and Chris Getty, a grandson of J. Paul Getty; the commodore and vice commodore of Britain's Royal Yacht Squadron: Lord Amherst and Sir Nigel Southward, Queen Elizabeth II's personal physician. Mr. Getty and I are the only crewmembers who haven't sailed across the Atlantic before.

After the start of the race, the wind was light and coming out of the northeast, forcing us to raise and lower sails that weigh several hundred pounds over and over again as we sought to find the optimal combination. We also had to adopt a much more easterly course than we had planned because of the direction of the wind—it was coming from pretty much exactly where we wanted to go—and also to keep close to *Maximus,* a just-launched "super-maxiyacht" that is our closest competition. During the early evening the wind picked up and we hit something closer to our stride, 18 knots, but *Maximus* was performing just as well. By 1 a.m., it was slightly ahead of us. But during the next several hours we began to pull ahead, and by mid-morning on Monday, *Maximus* was seven miles behind and barely visible.

Mr. Miller was a happy man when he came on deck

that morning to hear the news about *Maximus*. He had also learned that *Mari-Cha* had traveled much farther than *Atlantic* had during the first hours of the 1905 race. It was also his 72nd birthday, which was celebrated with a granola bar that had held a pair of burning matchsticks.

The day began quietly. After I went on deck for my early morning shift, the sky was illuminated by a full moon on one side, a glow from where the sun would rise on the other side, and a vast electrical storm stretching across the horizon directly ahead of us. Within a few hours, the wind began to build—and with it the waves. By late afternoon, the wind was gusting up to 47 knots. I was grateful that we had so many around-the-world sailors onboard. As waves crashed over the deck, they did most of the work as we reefed the mainsail and replaced our genoa with a much smaller sail.

The direction of the wind had also changed, so, for the first time, it was not coming from the direction we needed to go. Surfing down the front of the waves, we briefly hit speeds of close to 40 knots and maintained a blistering pace throughout the night and on Tuesday. *Maximus* could not keep up. By Wednesday morning it had fallen 70 miles behind us.

Given the constant activity and our sleep patterns, it is difficult to remember what time—or even day —it is. But there is no confusion about what we have to do: We have to reach the English Channel in the next few days so we can beat *Atlantic*'s record.

# A Hard-Won Victory at Sea

*The Wall Street Journal*
*June 2, 2005*

NEAR LAND'S END, ENGLAND—We made it! Shortly after 10 a.m. yesterday (U.K. time), *Mari-Cha IV* crossed a line near the start of the English Channel to break Charlie Barr's 100-year-old transatlantic racing record of 12 days, four hours, one minute and 19 seconds. We completed the almost 3,000-mile course in nine days, 15 hours, 55 minutes and 23 seconds, shaving more than two days from Barr's legendary record.

It was not easy. During the first days of the race, we headed almost directly into the wind and waves, conditions that we believed to be favorable to *Maximus,* our closest competitor. Then on the night of Wednesday,

May 25, as we approached Grand Banks off Newfound-land amid gale-force winds, we suffered a series of breakages that very nearly forced us to withdraw from the race.

First off, our genoa, the forward-most sail, separated from the line that held it to the top of the mast, forcing the crew to wrestle the sail to the deck and replace it with a much smaller sail. Then, as the wind gusted up to 50 knots, the mainsail, the boat's most important, began to part from the vessel. The 3,200-square-foot sail is connected to 14 "cars," which slide up and down an aluminum track that is bolted to the mast. After the bow launched off a steep 15-foot wave and returned to the water with an explosive crash, the upper-most car disintegrated and a section of the track began to lift away from the mast. The $300,000 sail was removed in less than five minutes, before the track totally self-destructed, but we were then effectively unable to continue racing.

Just before midnight, Bob Miller, *Mari-Cha*'s owner, said, "The ghost of Charlie Barr must be smiling."

A few minutes after that, another major problem arose: The track on the other mast, the mizzen mast, also started peeling away. By then, many, maybe most, of our crew, which includes several of the world's top-rated professional sailors, had concluded that we should withdraw from the race. It had been the most difficult transatlantic crossing anyone aboard had experienced, morale was terrible, and further damage seemed likely. Most of us thought that repairs, even if they could be made, would leave us too compromised to really compete.

Mr. Miller would not hear of it. "I don't want to retire," he said to Mike Sanderson and Jef d'Etiveaud, his top crewmen, early Thursday morning. "That has to be our very last option."

By daybreak Thursday, *Maximus* had erased our lead and pulled ahead by about 30 miles. With just two small sails, we were moving at less than 10 knots. We had developed a multipronged plan of attack to reverse the damage, but we could not do anything until the wind and waves diminished to the point that crewmen could be hoisted up the masts.

At 11:30 a.m., when the breeze dropped to about 15 knots, Justin Clougher and Francis Tregaskis went up the main mast carrying an electric drill and a power cord that had been assembled using every one of the vessel's extension cords. Once they were 90 feet above the deck, they struggled to drill seven holes through the track and into mast as they were being knocked into and away from the mast.

Meanwhile, Damien Durchon and Jeremy Lomas went up the mizzen mast. While they bore holes and drove a dozen screws into that mast, other members of the crew used patches and polyurethane glue to repair tears that had developed in the sails.

At 4 p.m., the repairs were complete and we resumed racing. By then, though, *Maximus* had expanded its lead to 45 miles. Mr. Sanderson thought we were unlikely to catch up. Our only hope was a wind shift that would play to *Mari-Cha*'s greatest strength—downwind sailing. "What we have to hope for is a southeasterly shift that comes before it's too late," Mr. Sanderson said.

On Sunday morning, almost a week after we left New York, we finally found a favorable breeze, a southeasterly with 20 knots. That is what *Mari-Cha* was built for, which became obvious as our speed accelerated to an exhilarating 20 knots. We have been moving at about that speed ever since, enabling us to reach the line in time and also maintain a comfortable lead over *Maximus,* which was about 40 miles behind us when we completed the race.

It has been a very long trip, quick enough to break the record but longer than most of us expected when we left New York a week and a half ago. But as we crossed the line in fog yesterday morning, the horrendous weather, the crippling problems with the boat, and the lousy food did not seem important anymore.

# Our Race to New York was No Pleasure Cruise

*The Wall Street Journal*
*May 10, 2006*

NEW YORK HARBOR—What a ride!

As we left Annapolis and headed toward the starting line for the sixth leg of the Volvo Ocean Race early Sunday afternoon, I was looking forward to a rapid sprint to New York aboard *ABN AMRO ONE,* which had won four of the five previous legs of the 32,000-nautical-mile around-the-world race. It didn't turn out that way.

Mike Sanderson, our skipper, who is universally called "Moose," had told us there was the potential for heavy weather. "We're going to have a pretty hellish night," he said during a pre-race briefing. "Between 2 and 4 a.m. on Monday, we could have 50 knot gusts." He asked the 10-man crew to fight hard. "We have a couple of days to sleep in New York, so let's give it hell for the next

30 hours." But he also issued a caution: "The most important thing is getting there in one piece. We have a lot to lose: If we break the boat and can't start in the next leg, that would be a total disaster."

At the start of the Annapolis to New York leg, the sun was shining and the wind was calm, about eight knots, providing a perfect day for the thousands of spectator boats that had come out to watch. But the wind was too gentle for "Black Betty," as *ABN AMRO ONE*'s crew calls its 70-foot rocket of a yacht. With its relatively wide hull, it performs better in heavy weather. Six of the other boats left us behind as the fleet headed south toward the mouth of the Chesapeake Bay, and by late afternoon two of them had disappeared into the distance.

That all changed Sunday evening when we were two thirds of our way down the Chesapeake and the wind picked up to 23 to 26 knots. With a push of a button, the 21-foot-long keel canted from side to side, enabling us to keep the boat relatively upright in spite of the force of the wind. Betty soon reached a speed identical to the wind's. It was as if someone ignited booster engines to hurtle us out to sea. By the time we crossed under the Chesapeake Bay Bridge and entered the Atlantic shortly after midnight, we had passed four of the other boats.

That's also when the real trouble began. The wind speed exceeded 30 knots and a series of squalls buffeted us with 42-knots. Worse, the breeze—and waves—were coming from the north, the direction we wanted to go. That meant Betty was repeatedly climbing

waves that were unseen except for the frothing white at
their peaks and then falling into the trough on the other
side, a scenario that can cause composite-hulled boats
to break. Remarkably, these were the most challenging conditions the crew had experienced in the seven-
month race. They had occasionally been hit by stronger wind, but this was the first time they had had such
powerful wind and waves on the nose.

During the very early hours of Monday morning,
Black Betty's deck became a war zone as the crew
battled rain and stinging sleet to reduce the size of the
sails. The bowmen, Jan Dekker and Justin Slattery, had
the toughest tasks. Twice they had to change our headsail—wrestling the sails down to the deck, keeping
track of lines in the darkness and hoisting replacement
sails while the hull crashed off the wavesand tons of
water washed over the deck. Several battle-hardened
sailors became seasick. No one slept until after 7 a.m.
Even then, it was only for catnaps and no one both-
ered to take off their foul-weather gear or boots when
they lay down on their bunks or on the floor. They knew
another sail change would soon require "all hands on
deck."

There's nothing like the Volvo (or the Whitbread, as
it was known until Volvo took over the sponsorship
reins in 2001). The current edition began when seven
yachts set out from Spain and headed south last November. After a stop in Cape Town, South Africa, the yachts
entered the treacherous Southern Ocean and circled
much of Antarctica, making stops in Australia and New

Zealand, before heading back north to Rio de Janeiro and then up to the Chesapeake.

I'm only onboard for this one leg—it's the first time journalists have been allowed to be onboard during the racing—but I already have a much greater appreciation for this event's extraordinary challenges. The conditions onboard, from the uncomfortable bunks to the open toilet and freeze-dried food, are Spartan, and the demands are constant. The only place to be is either on deck or lying down in the carbon-fiber black cabin. The only thing that resembles a chair is the swing-like seat where Stan Honey, the navigator, somehow manages to avoid seasickness as he works with a pair of computers and weather information to plot the optimal course.

Black Betty can reach incredible speeds. Earlier in the race, between Spain and South Africa, it sailed 546 miles in a single day. We couldn't achieve anything like that while heading into the south-bound wind and waves. The wind direction also meant that we had to repeatedly tack back and forth. With each tack, we lost a quarter of a mile. And each turn meant that hundreds of pounds of sails had to be shifted from one side of the boat to the other.

But we were doing better than our competitors. When we received data about the other boats' positions on Monday morning, we learned that we were ahead of them all.

As the sun set Monday night, we were tacking back and forth up the New Jersey coastline, which was sometimes visible. The wind was still strong, averaging 27 knots, and our lead expanded through the night. But Moose, who had slept only a few minutes since the start, was not taking anything for granted even after we passed Ambrose Light and made our way toward the bright lights of the Verrazano Narrows Bridge and, beyond that, the Statue of Liberty.

Only when we crossed the finish line near the southern tip of Manhattan at 4:06 a.m. and learned that the closest of the other boats still had 23 miles to go did our skipper break into a smile. Shaking hands with everyone on his crew, he said, "Nice work guys—that was a real toughie of a race, so this is a particularly sweet victory."

Despite the hour, spectators and champagne were waiting on the dock, but the crew will not have long to savor its victory. The seventh leg, from New York to Portsmouth, England, begins tomorrow.

# Olin Stephen's Radical Yacht

*The Wall Street Journal*
*November 4, 2006*

Olin Stephen's obsession with sailboats took hold shortly after World War I during a childhood visit to Cape Cod. He didn't just admire them. He studied them with what he later described as "great concentration," sketching any he thought might be worth emulating and imagining how he might do things differently.

By the time he was 20, Mr. Stephens had dropped out of M.I.T., had brief apprenticeships with several leading yacht designers, drawn up plans for a handful of small boats, and formed his own company, Sparkman & Stephens. On the basis of Olin's early promise, his father, who had recently sold the family coal-supply business, placed an order for a relatively large yacht, a 52-foot yawl.

When *Dorade,* named for the dolphin that is correctly spelled Dorado, was launched in 1931, it sparked a revolution.

It was strikingly slender, its beam just 10-foot-3. It was also, by the standards of the day, extremely lightweight, in part because the frames that supported the hull were made from steam-bent sections of wood weighing far less than conventional and much bulkier sawn frames. Until then, it was believed that ocean-going stability could not be achieved without a much broader and heavier hull. *Dorade*'s stability came from a different source—a lengthy lead keel that put the ballast far below the waterline, where it would be much more effective in counterbalancing the force of the wind.

Thanks to the combination of a streamlined hull and "outside ballast," Mr. Stephens was confident that his creation would be fast. It was also strikingly beautiful. Like most designers of that time, he believed boats that were pleasing to the eye were also faster than unattractive ones. *Dorade*'s bow and stern rose from the water with curvaceous grace, creating the elegant overhangs that are hallmarks of classic sailing yachts.

But *Dorade* represented a major risk. Mr. Stephens had created a radical new design without the computer analysis and tank testing that is now commonplace. He had relied upon instincts alone, intuitive judgments of how the vessel's lines would affect its performance. The lack of precision was obvious the moment *Dorade* was launched: The white stripe that had been painted around the hull to mark the waterline disappeared as it sank three inches below the surface. When Mr. Stephens announced that he was going to enter *Dorade* in a transatlantic race, many yachtsmen thought he was foolhardy.

Mr. Stephens was the skipper and navigator during the race, which set out for England from Newport, R.I., on July 4, 1931. His seven-man crew, which included his younger brother Rod, who had overseen the yacht's construction and would become a partner in Sparkman & Stephens, was young: Even with the inclusion of the Mr. Stephens's 46-year-old father, the average age was just 22.

Olin Stephens was at the helm when *Dorade* crossed the finish line on July 31. Longer sailboats generally go faster than shorter ones, but *Dorade,* the third smallest of the 10-yacht fleet, reached the line more than two days before the second-place boat. When the times were handicapped, or "corrected," to reflect the differences among the yachts, *Dorade*'s time was almost four days better than its closest rival. *Dorade* went on to win the Fastnet Race by a wide margin. When the crew returned to New York City, where Sparkman & Stephens had its office, they were rewarded with a ticker-tape parade, a first for sailors.

And yacht design would never be the same. The assumptions that had limited naval architects to incremental advances were abandoned and the modern age of racing design, defined by an endless quest to produce lighter but more powerful yachts, commenced. No one benefited from this more than Mr. Stephens, who became the most successful designer of the 20th century, creating plans for six successful America's Cup defenders, two of which were two-time winners.

*Dorade* also became a legend. The Stephens family sold it in 1936, but successor owners have underwritten the ceaseless work of maintaining an aging wooden vessel. In recent years, it was based in the Mediterranean, where an Italian owner competed in Europe's active classic yacht racing circuit. But since it was acquired by Edgar Cato, an accomplished American yachtsman, about a year ago, it has been based in Newport. "It was a piece of history that I had read about for most of my life—and I decided that I wanted to bring it back to the United States," Mr. Cato told me.

Over Labor Day weekend, he and Mr. Stephens, now 98 but still traveling to yachting events around the world from his home in Hanover, N.H., boarded *Dorade* to compete in the Museum of Yachting's annual Classic Yacht Regatta in Narragansett Bay. Although Mr. Stephens himself advised the crew on the most favorable sail combinations, *Dorade* placed second after a section of the rigging failed in winds gusting to more than 30 knots. "We would have won otherwise," said Mr. Cato, who plans to continue racing *Dorade* in the Caribbean and New England.

Unfailingly modest, Mr. Stephens is reluctant to rate *Dorade* as a masterpiece. When I spoke to him a couple of weeks ago, he said it was too narrow, that it would go even faster, and be less "rolly," if he had given it just a bit more breadth. But he acknowledged that Dorade was a breakthrough—or, as he put it, "a kind of awak-ening"—for yachting design. "I knew that a lighter boat with outside ballast was the way to go, and that a deep and narrow hull would go through the sea nicely. It was obvious. It was like taking candy from a baby. It just had to win."

# Sir Robin's Latest Circumnavigation

*The Wall Street Journal*
*April 18, 2007*

In 1969, the same year Neil Armstrong landed on the moon, Robin Knox-Johnston completed the first nonstop solo circumnavigation of planet Earth. Now, at age 68, he is making another solo lap around the globe as part of the Velux 5 Oceans race. Of the seven men who started, two have dropped out, and Sir Robin is currently in fourth place.

Unlike the circumnavigation that turned a young seaman into a maritime legend and earned him a knighthood, this race, which set out from Bilbao, Spain, on October 22, includes two scheduled stops, first in Fremantle, Western Australia, and then in Norfolk, Va. Sir Robin did reasonably well on the first leg, finishing in third place, but the second was, as he puts it, "a bit of a nightmare." First, the automatic pilot malfunctioned shortly after he left Fremantle, forcing him to return to port for repairs. Then, just as he was entering the Southern Ocean, both of the satellite phone systems through which he received weather information failed. Finally, the device that is supposed to hold the mainsail to the top of the 84-foot mast came apart, making it impossible for him to fully raise his most important sail.

Despite all of this, he was still holding onto third place as he neared Cape Horn, but the accumulation of problems forced him to make another unscheduled pit stop in Southern Argentina. And once he resumed racing, he became mired in the Doldrums. On March 8, when there were still 4,719 nautical miles between him and Norfolk, there was so little wind that Sir Robin went swimming and used dish-washing liquid to wash himself. "I find it best not to think about the race—it's too depressing," he wrote in his daily blog. By the time he reached Norfolk on March 30, he had fallen to fourth place, almost two full days behind the third-place finisher, Unai Basurko, a 32-year-old Spaniard. Sir Robin was bitterly disappointed.

"I'm not here just to finish," he told me a few days ago. "I want to be up there—I want to do well."

Sir Robin did not come from a family of mariners, but he knew that he wanted to go to sea from early childhood; he became a merchant mariner after he failed the Royal Navy's entrance examination. He has always been a determined competitor. Until he completed his nonstop circumnavigation as part of a challenge sponsored by London's *Sunday Times,* it was widely believed to be an impossible feat. He was the only one of nine men who entered the contest to finish, and he went on to chalk up a host of other victories and firsts. In 1994, he teamed up with Sir Peter Blake, another legendary sailor, to win the Jules Verne trophy by sailing around the world on a catamaran in just 74 days.

"I'm a great believer in competitive sports," Sir Robin told me, making it clear that he abhors the notion that children should be praised for their athletic performances irrespective of how well they do. "You can't always win—life is competitive—but losing teaches you something too."

He says he entered the Velux 5 Oceans Race to prove that he, despite the passing of decades, can continue to play his game and not just the seniors' version. He called his boat *Grey Power* until he renamed it *Saga Insurance* in recognition of his principal sponsor, a company that specializes in selling financial products to Britons who are 50 or more years old. "Just because you turn 65, doesn't mean your brain turns to porridge and you can't do anything anymore," he declares.

Some have suggested that Sir Robin's participation was financially driven because a company he runs owns the rights to the race, but he says his motivation is rooted in more meaningful things and has a lot to do with the death of his wife, Suzanne, four years ago. His habit of "wandering off" for lengthy nautical adventures had led her to divorce him, resulting in a seven-year separation. But the couple, friends since childhood, later remarried to resume what he now describes as a storybook marriage. "The mourning process is a peculiar thing," he says. "I needed to draw a line."

The race's final leg will begin today. Sir Robin already knows he has no chance of winning the race, but he desperately wants to earn back his third place position by the time he reaches Spain. It will not be easy. He is 41 hours behind the Spaniard, a sizable deficit to overcome during a transatlantic crossing.

The day-to-day reality of the race is a lot different from Sir Robin's first trip around the world, an odyssey that was more about survival than speed and that took 313 days. He was aboard *Suhaili,* a 32-foot wooden ketch he'd had built in Bombay when he was based there as a merchant mariner. *Suhaili* and *Saga Insurance* both weigh about nine tons, but the newer vessel, thanks to the wonders of carbon fiber, is twice as long, and it carries sails four times as large. It can maintain speeds of 15 knots or more and hit 30 when riding a wave. *Suhaili* averaged four knots and rarely did better than seven.

Satellite communications is the other big change. On *Suhaili,* Sir Robin had to spend two hours every day working with his sextant just to determine where he was. Because his radio broke down early in the race, no one knew where he was for months at a time. If something had gone wrong, no one would have known. This time a global positioning system effortlessly calculates his position, distress beacons are ready to emit signals that would be heard around the world, and he has satellite telephones.

The technological enhancements have done nothing to provide for a more comfortable ride. The endless challenges of maximizing speed are both physical and strategic—"chess with chin-ups," as Sir Robin puts it. There is never enough time for sleep. When he does, it is rarely longer than 90 minutes at a stretch, and it is usually on a narrow bench next to the navigational equipment. There is no toilet, only a bucket. Almost all of the food is freeze dried, the main exception being several bottles of Gentleman's Relish, a fish paste made mostly from anchovies, which he spreads on crackers when he decides he has done something worthy of celebrating.

Actually, Sir Robin allows himself one other treat—alcohol. Unique among the competitors, his yacht carries a supply of scotch and several two-liter cartons of wine, both white and red. When conditions allow, he sits down between 5 p.m. and 6 p.m., glass in hand, and reflects upon the day's accomplishments.

# Personal Vendetta

*Showboats Magazine*
*March 2008*

OYSTER BAY—Billy Joel had two great loves when he was young, classical music and boats. The boats came first. Growing up near the center of Long Island in middle class Hicksville, the highlight of his childhood weekends was visits to Jones Beach and this community on the North Shore. He preferred Oyster Bay because it was populated by boats. He did not know anyone who actually owned a boat, but he dreamed about them and spent an inordinate amount of his time at school sketching out their profiles. When he was twelve, he started "borrowing" untended skiffs. He always returned them—he says he sometimes even cleaned them up a bit—and he kept coming back for more. For reasons he could not explain, the feeling of being on the water was close to magical.

Several decades later, the pull is just as strong, but Joel now has several boats of his own, including *Vendetta,* a fifty-seven-foot "commuter boat." An immaculately maintained black-hulled beauty, it has the same classic lines as the original commuters that sped J.P. Morgan, Jr. and other Wall Street tycoons between their North Shore mansions and Manhattan.

Joel was wearing a black tee-shirt, dark green shorts and black boat shoes on a pleasant summer morning when he arrived at the Hudson River marina where *Vendetta* was secured to a dock. The only thing he was carrying was Sabrina, one of his two pet pugs. Shortly after he climbed aboard, his captain, Gene Pelland, guided the vessel away from the dock. "It's kind of noisy," Joel warned. A few minutes later, we were barreling down the Hudson at a loud but exhilarating forty-four knots. Sabrina fell asleep in a leather-covered captain's chair.

Joel is very proud of his boat, which he launched in 2005. The design work began with drawings he made several years earlier. "My only parameters were that it had to go fast and look great," he told me. Joel faxed his first drawings to Pelland, who worked as a carpenter building stages when Joel was on tour. Pelland passed them along to Doug Zurn, the naval architect who turned them into more detailed plans, which Pelland sometimes tacked to dressing room walls before Joel's performances. "He'd say, 'That looks good, but it needs a bit of this or that," Pelland remembers. "Billy had this boat in his head for a long time—it's all him."

As we rounded the southern end of Manhattan, Joel marveled at the skyline and the East River bridges that were lined up in front of us. "When you see this panorama from the water, you understand why Manhattan became such an important place."

Just after we passed under the Brooklyn Bridge, he noticed a small Coast Guard patrol boat that appeared to be chasing us. It could not begin to match our speed, so Joel told Pelland to slow down. When the Coast Guardsmen were so close that they may have recognized the Piano Man, they waved us on. Having bowed to the authorities, Joel then seemed eager to demonstrate that the guy who used to borrow boats has not lost his sense of mischief. Pointing toward the FDR Drive, where traffic was moving at about the same pace as we were, he said, "When it's really backed up, we slow down and kind of give them a wave. Then we put the hammer down. They hate us!"

After *Vendetta* entered Long Island Sound, Joel talked about the original commuter boat owners. "These tycoons—they put aircraft engines on their boats and they used to have races on the way to Manhattan." Joel says he spends one out of every four days on one of his boats but that he has a problem: "I don't have to work during the week, but most of my friends do. I need some more rich friends, so I have people to play hooky with."

Joel started traveling back and forth to New York by boat back in the 1970s after he bought his first house on Oyster Bay, a waterfront home on Lloyd Neck he shared with Christie Brinkley. In those days, he had a relatively modest twenty-foot-fishing boat. When *Vendetta* headed into Oyster Bay, we passed that house and entered Joel's favorite piece of water. The first section of the bay is also known as Cold Spring Harbor, the name he gave to his first solo album. Shortly after we sped past the house on Lloyd Neck, we could see another one of his former houses, a modern-looking structure with big windows that appeared on the cover of his "Glass Houses" album. Then we passed one of the commercial oyster dredges on which Joel worked when he was a teenager. A minute later, we were approaching his current home, a large Georgian Revival style mansion on Centre Island, a narrow stretch of land situated in the middle of the bay.

"I remember seeing that house when I was a kid," Joel said. "I thought it was a castle that belonged to a duke or a marquis or something. Now I own it." Those words probably make it sound like Joel was bragging. Maybe he was, but it didn't sound like that to me. I think what he was actually trying to say was that the boy from Hicksville still finds it rather incredible that his biggest childhood dreams have turned true.

We reached the dock seventy-five minutes after we left the marina in Manhattan. While Joel was pleased by the time, his satisfaction came from the speed itself, not because he was in a rush. When he got off the boat, he just stood on the dock, admiring the bay and his creation. He also explained why he named it *Vendetta*. "It comes from that saying—living well is the best revenge." When I asked, "Revenge for what?" he laughed.

"There's a long list. First of all, the IRS. Then the people who said I couldn't sing. Then the people who said a guy from Hicksville couldn't be a rock star. And the people who said I couldn't marry Christie Brinkley." Finally, as he motioned his hand toward his house, he added, "And for all the people who said I couldn't own a house like that one."

# Steeped in Ambition

*The Wall Street Journal*
*July 9, 2010*

When I interviewed Larry Ellison prior to the most recent competition for the America's Cup, I put forth the proposition that if he prevailed (which he did) that the first words of his obituary might be focused on the Cup rather than Oracle Corporation, the giant software company he founded. Ellison did not disagree. "Oracle could disappear someday," he said. "The America's Cup will not."

Sir Thomas Lipton, who died in 1931, created the first large chain of grocery stores as well as the tea business that still carries his name, but he probably is remembered most for his epic pursuit of the Cup. Even though all five of his campaigns were unsuccessful, they did much to turn him into the world's first business-man-celebrity—a showman-entrepreneur not unlike Donald Trump.

Lipton's quest for sailing's greatest prize did not begin until he was 50, and Michael D'Antonio does not get around to describing it until near the middle of his captivating book, "A Full Cup." That is as it should be. The book's most compelling passages explore the origins of Lipton's genius as a marketer, not just of products but also of himself. When his Irish immigrant parents operated a small food store in a Glasgow slum, he told his mother she should always be the one to offer up the eggs because they looked larger in her delicate hands. When he took on a local bully and kept fighting long after it became obvious to a crowd of neighborhood boys that he could not win, he learned that perceptions can be built on singular demonstrations of character—that it is possible to succeed without actually winning.

In 1866, when Lipton was just 17, he traveled to New York where, after a few false starts, he found a job with one of the first department stores. There he saw how "a bit of polish and a smattering of pleasant conversation created what he called an 'atmosphere.'" His responsibilities grew quickly, but a few years later he returned to Glasgow where he opened his own grocery store on his 23rd birthday.

Riding a pair of mighty waves—a rapidly emerging middle class and falling wholesale prices—he ultimately built almost 300 stores. Nonstop, frequently humorous promotion was his hallmark. He sometimes hired a dozen or so overweight men and a similar number of "cadaverous males" and had them march down opposite sides of busy shopping streets. The thin men carried signs saying, "Going to Lipton's;" the signs on the more rounded men read, "Coming from Lipton's."

Lipton seemed to make all the right moves and there are few flaws in Mr. D'Antonio's nicely crafted volume. He introduces a sufficient number of contemporaneous characters, everyone from Teddy Roosevelt and J.P. Morgan to Oscar Wilde, to set the historical scene, but not so many as to bog down the story. Less impressive are the accounts of Lipton's America's Cup challenges, which took place from 1899 to 1929. They are thin and in places awkward. Sailors will find it odd to hear Cup races called "heats."

But the book's only significant shortcoming is its frustrating—but for the most part understandable—gaps regarding Lipton's personal life. He was a gregarious bon vivant, and his friends included King Edward and Thomas Edison and many of the other best known figures from both sides of the Atlantic. But he never dated a woman or shared a home with anyone other than his parents, who lived with him until their deaths, and a close male friend who also became his company's second in command. Mr. D'Antonio suggests that their relationship was romantic, but we do not know for sure.

We also never learn what drove Lipton's ambition. Lipton named all of his businesses for himself, and he once undertook a Trump-like effort to put his name on every one of the navigational buoys that marked

Glasgow's bustling harbor. Was this ego? Or was he was simply seeking to link his products to his own persona, which had become his most valuable creation?

Lipton's participation in the America's Cup—then the world's biggest sporting event—may well have started as a part of his promotional efforts, a kind of transoceanic reputational brand extension. He had, after all, never before owned a boat, he knew next to nothing about sailing, and he was never onboard during races. But over the course of his 30-year quest, which continued until he died, it seems likely that it took on some emotional importance. How much? The author is unable to say.

Lipton always had an extraordinary sense of timing. By the time he died, in 1931, the Great Depression was deepening and giant yachts were becoming an unaffordable luxury. "As much as any man, Thomas Lipton had lived the story of the Gilded Age," Mr. D'Antonio tells us. "Hard years of economic retrenchment, resentment and recrimination were at hand. Sir Thomas Lipton would face none of it."

# The Seafarer

The Wall Street Journal
October 23, 2010

Joshua Slocum is remembered for two things—
being the first person to sail single-handedly around the
world and for his marvelous account of the journey. In his
biography of Slocum, "The Hard Way Around," Geoffrey
Wolff focuses less on the nautical and literary achievements than on what Slocum did before.

For the most part, it is not a pretty picture. *The
New York Times* called Slocum a barbarian after he was
imprisoned for allegedly mistreating a sailor. On one of
the vessels he commanded, several crewmen contract-
ed smallpox and Slocum was arrested again, this time
for killing a mutinous member of the crew. Although
he eventually resumed command of the ship, it then
went aground and was lost in Brazil. By age 45, two of

the ships he commanded had been wrecked, his first wife and three of his children had died, and he was unemployed and broke.

I confess that, halfway into this seemingly endless tale of woe, I was thinking about jumping ship myself. The early chapters are slow-moving, especially for readers who may have anticipated an adventure story. There are also some odd changeups in style, from carefully considered, grown-up prose to juvenile sentences such as this one: "It was a miracle the hulk didn't sink, though if you wait a bit, she will.'"

In truth, Mr. Wolff's writing was not my main problem. I was troubled by his overall approach, what in places seemed like an almost sneering disrespect for his subject. Slocum's solo-circumnavigation—he set out from Boston 1895 and arrived back in Newport, R.I. in June 1898—was an extraordinary feat, and his book, "Sailing Alone Around the World," is an intoxicating masterpiece. I saw little purpose in dwelling on Slocum's failings.

But I kept reading, mostly because of Wolff's engaging description of what it was like to be a mariner during the great age of sail. Slocum was 16 when he went to sea in 1860. He wanted to command one of the tall-masted clipper ships, and once he achieved his objective, ten years later, he didn't just chart the course and direct the crew. He also functioned as the ship's resident entrepreneur, identifying cargos to carry and negotiating the terms. He called on exotic ports throughout the world, with his wife and children onboard most of the time.

But Slocum was born too late. The clipper ship era is probably the most celebrated period of marine history, the inspiration for the dramatic seascapes that hang in hotel lobbies and stodgy clubs everywhere. But it didn't last long. Even in 1860, wood-hulled sailing vessels were being displaced by steel ships that were powered by steam. By the time Slocum took command of his most impressive ship, the 233-foot-long *Northern Lights*, in 1881, the tide was flowing swiftly against the clippers.

Ultimately, it is in the attempt to connect Slocum's circumstances and his choices to his failures and his immortalizing achievements that Wolff's finds bookworthy purpose. After Slocum lost his ship in Brazil in 1887, he built a 35-foot "sailing canoe" and set out on a 5,000-mile journey back to the U.S., this time with his second wife Hettie (his first wife, Virginia, had died three years before), and two of his children, one of them a toddler. This is how Slocum, in his book, explained the switch to small-boat sailing: "The old boating trick came back fresh to me, the love of the thing itself gaining on me as the little ship stood out; and my crew with one voice said, 'Go on.'"

Not far into the journey, the little boat ran into a squall and the sails, which had been sewn by Hettie, shredded. Seeking to answer the question of what Slocum was thinking at such times, Mr. Wolff bores into Slocum's prose like a literary detective. Of Slocum's lifetime sailing obsession and his arresting phrase "the love of the thing itself," he wrote that it came from "irreducible, hard-nut recognition and radiant sentiment."

Wolff doesn't get around to describing Slocum's 46,000-mile lap around the planet until his book's penultimate chapter. By then, many readers are likely to be so intrigued by the man and the great why-he-did-it question that they will be eager to read Slocum's own book—which is as it should be. Slocum's masterpiece has never gone out of print.

What is it that drives some people to undertake the audacious? We live at time when many of the most important firsts have already been claimed, but people seem more obsessed than ever with establishing records, some of them of dubious distinction. Businessmen-climbers search for mountain peaks that have never been surmounted, marathoners go to Antarctica to run, and a recent procession of teenagers have sought to replicate Slocum's circumnavigation (with the benefit of high-tech boats, push-button navigational equipment, and satellite telephones).

Was Slocum like these people? Before I read Wolff's book, I would have said no, that his motives and achievement were more pure and singular. Now I am unsure. Many modern-day adventurers are driven by ego. And ego might have played a role with Slocum, who may have been eager to demonstrate that he was, in spite of his setbacks, exceptionally skilled at what he did to the point, as he put it, of "neglecting all else." And aren't some contemporary adventurers individuals who, like Slocum, feel like they have run out of other options?

Then again, perhaps Slocum was unique. Maybe it really was all about "the thing itself." In November of 1908, he sailed from his home on Martha's Vineyard to undertake an unheralded solo exploration of the Venezuelan coast and the Amazon. Somewhere along the way he disappeared. No one knows what happened.

# Aboard the Spindrift

*Rhapsody Magazine*
*March 2014*

LORIENT, FRANCE—When Christopher Columbus sailed from Spain to the Bahamas in 1492, it took ten weeks. Last October, Dona Bertarelli and Yann Guichard sailed a nearly identical 3,885-mile route aboard their maxi trimaran, *Spindrift 2,* in less than one, besting the previous record for what sailors call the Discovery Route by more than 20 hours.

A few weeks earlier, I joined the boat's crew in France as they prepared for their attempt at the record.

Sunrise was still an hour away when I arrived on the dock, so it was difficult to see much. *Spindrift*'s three 131-foot-long hulls and its towering mast were jet black, as were the uniforms of the crewmen, who moved about with the help of head-mounted flashlights.

Named for the spray of water launched by the hulls as they charge through the sea at speeds that were, until recently inconceivable for a large sail-powered vessel, *Spindrift,* is as fast as the hydro-foiling catamarans that began racing for the America's Cup in San Francisco Bay the week I arrived in Lorient. And it has far greater endurance: In 2012, its previous owner sailed it around the world in an astonishing 45 days.

The goal for this day was to perfect various techniques and enhance the crew's cohesiveness. Once we cleared the harbor, when the wind speed was 12 knots, Guichard asked the 14-person crew to raise the 4,800-square-foot mainsail and a smaller headsail. As the sails filled, the port hull levitated from the water and we accelerated rapidly. We were soon moving at twice the speed of the wind. If that's a concept that's difficult to grasp, another fact of super-fast sailing was all too apparent: You do not want to fall off the boat. "After two minutes in the water, it would be impossible to see the person in the water," said Bertarelli, a billioniare heiress, whose brother Ernesto led the Swiss team Alinghi to win the America's Cup in 2003 and 2007. "After five, that person wouldn't be able to see the boat."

As we sailed away from the coast, we were moving so quickly that birds could not begin to keep pace, and before long, we had lost sight of land. When we were 28 miles off the coast, Guichard turned the helm over to me.

The basic task of steering *Spindrift*—maintaining a course that took us generally where we wanted to go while taking maximum advantage of the wind—was fundamentally no different than on any boat, but the extraordinary speed meant that I had to rely on a digital readout of the wind's direction rather than traditional indicators. *Spindrift*'s speed was intoxicating—though it inevitably led to a desire for even more. I could not resist making frequent checks of another digital indicator, the one showing our speed. I was able to keep it close to 30 knots, and at one point I got it up to 35.4—or 41 miles per hour—which turned out, to my great surprise, to be our top speed of the day.

The speed produced a cacophony of sound. The shrouds were not just whistling but also were causing sections of the boat's carbon-fiber structure to vibrate. The decking on which I was standing produced a continuous—and somewhat alarming—thumping noise, which I also felt through the soles of my shoes.

An even more arresting sound sometimes came from the rudder mounted on the back of the hull nearest to me. When I was doing my job well, this hull and the entire length of the rudder flew above the water. When I slipped up, the hull dropped down a bit and the rudder pierced the surface of the water, producing a loud hiss that sounded just like that of an angry cat. It was a sound I found satisfying—more dramatically than the digital speed indicator, it gave proof to our remarkable pace—but it also seemed a bit like chastisement, or perhaps a warning.

There is no getting around the fact that *Spindrift*'s speed carries risk. Things could go wrong, in seconds. Structural elements could break. *What was causing that thumping?* And then there is the ultimate fear: The boat could capsize.

In June, Guichard was racing another boat owned by Bertarelli, a 70-foot trimaran, off the coast of Ireland when a sudden gust caused it to overturn. The mast crumbled and a member of the crew, Guichard's brother Jacques, suffered a broken pelvis.

Not long after I gave up the helm, we had a close call of our own. It came after the wind gusted from 18 knots to 33, which caused the windward hull to rise much too far above the water. The crewman who should have released the headsail had not done so, so the boat tipped further and further until the mast was a scary 21 degrees beyond vertical. Guichard, who was at the wheel, was unable to steer. *Spindrift* was completely out of control. Guichard has a reputation for never losing his cool, but he was obviously alarmed as he shouted instructions and struggled to pull at the wheel in a futile attempt to turn toward the source of the wind.

After what seemed like forever but was only a matter of seconds, the headsail was finally eased, and the hulls fell back toward the water. Catastrophe was averted. Nobody spoke about the incident until later, when we were back at the dock and Guichard spoke about the day's lessons learned, but it was a haunting moment, at least for me. Bertarelli chose to focus on the positives.

"On this boat, you can actually feel the acceleration," she said. "There's a kind of kick—and that's something you just don't get on a traditional monohull sailboat. You actually have the sense of flight."

**G. BRUCE KNECHT,** a former staff reporter and foreign correspondent for *The Wall Street Journal,* is the author of three books: *THE PROVING GROUND: The Inside Story of the 1998 Sydney to Hobart Race; HOOKED: Pirates, Poaching and the Perfect Fish;* and *GRAND AMBITION: An Extraordinary Yacht, the People Who Built It, and the Millionaire Who Can't Really Afford It.* He has also written for *The Atlantic, The New York Times Magazine, Smithsonian,* and *Conde Nast Traveler.* An avid sailor, Knecht raced across the Atlantic in 2005 on the yacht that broke the 100-year-old transatlantic race record. He lives in New York City.

**www.gbruceknecht.com**

Made in the USA
Middletown, DE
12 May 2017